Eternally
Desired

Living Out
Your Value in Yeshua

Miriam Nadler

All Hebrew and Greek words transliterated are in italics.

Book layout and cover design by Natalia Fomin

Eternally Desired by Miriam Nadler
© *2014, 2017 by Miriam Nadler*
All Rights Reserved
Printed in United States of America
ISBN: 978-1-530508112

Table of Contents

Foreword 5

Ancient Jewish Wedding Customs 6

1. You are His Chosen 13

2. While we are waiting 35

3. Living in Readiness 51

4. The Ultimate Celebration 65

5. The Song of Love 81

6. The Essence of Worship 101

Foreword

Eternally Desired is written from a Messianic Jewish frame of reference. Therefore, I utilized Messianic terms such as Yeshua which is Jesus in Hebrew, Messiah which is the equivalent of Christ and the Hebrew name Miriam for Mary. I also included some Hebrew words, with their meanings to enhance the understanding of the Scriptures.

A special thanks of appreciation to my husband, Sam, whose ongoing support encourages me to keep studying and writing. As this book was created my faith and confidence grew in the Word of God and the realization of His great love for each of us who trust in Yeshua.

Thank you to Natalia Fomin who is a respected teacher of the Word. Together we developed this teaching which parallels the Jewish Wedding customs and Messiah's relationship to us, His Bride.

Last but not least, a grateful thanks goes out to the women of Hope of Israel Congregation in Charlotte, NC who gave me their valuable feedback as we learned together our value in Yeshua.

My prayer is that this material will be faith building to each one who reads this book. I pray you will grow deeper in your love for your Beloved, Messiah Yeshua.

In His Grace,

Miriam Nadler

PS Thank you Shari Belfer for the use of your Ketubah on page 11 and for your last minute edits.

Ancient Jewish Wedding Customs

Before We Begin

The Scriptures are filled with earthly teaching symbols and ceremonies that God has given us to communicate His eternal truth. Since a wedding is one of the most joyful events in life, it serves as a great way to understand the joy, provision, and security of His kind intentions toward those who are in Messiah.

The title of this book, *Eternally Desired*, is about you and your importance to God. We will explore the steps of the ancient Jewish wedding customs and parallel them with Scripture. The symbol of the bride of Messiah and the wedding ceremony is woven throughout the fabric of the Hebrew Scriptures and the New Covenant. Paul describes this metaphor of marriage as a "mystery" in Ephesians 5:32, "This mystery is great; but I am speaking with reference to Messiah and the congregation."

The Scriptural simile of marriage is not new because throughout the Old Testament God expressed His relentless love towards the Jewish people, utilizing the metaphor of Israel as His wife and He as the husband. We will discover in the New Testament that the symbol of marriage takes a dramatic turn as Messiah Himself is described as the groom and His followers are called His bride.

Each chapter of this book will focus on a different aspect of Messiah, the groom, and His bride. We will consider an overview of the Ancient Jewish steps and parallel them with the Bride of Messiah from the New Covenant perspective. In the first chapter the emphasis is on His chosen bride. The second chapter gives insight as to what God expects of us as we wait for His return. In chapter three we look forward to that time when we will be taken to the wedding ceremony. Chapter four brings us to our heavenly home and a time of rejoicing with our groom. The concluding chapters will focus on the heart of the matter for now and eternity; the worship of our Eternal Groom.

The Scriptures define the Bride of Messiah as all believers in Yeshua, from the Feast of Pentecost until we meet Him in the air (Thessalonians 4:16). As His bride, each one of us is eternally desired by Him. For it was in eternity past where God first chose you and selected you to be His bride. The mystery of God's plan for us as His Bride is being unveiled the closer we get to see Him face to face. Your groom, Yeshua, has chosen you to be His own special treasure. My prayer is that by the end of this book, you will be fully convinced of your inestimable value in

Before We Begin

Him, and as a result you will fall more deeply in love with Yeshua and will share His love with others. The ancient Jewish wedding customs offer striking similarities with the mystery of the Bride of Messiah and her Groom, Yeshua.

Therefore, in order to understand these blessings in the heavenly places in Messiah, we will consider marriage from a heavenly perspective. Since God is the author of marriage throughout the Scriptures, He uses this example to speak of His relationship, first to Israel, then to the body of Messiah. Let's look at each one of the ancient Jewish wedding steps to discover how every stage parallels to a different aspect of our relationship to Messiah. These steps vary in some way from generation to generation. The following steps are referenced in the Scriptures: the arrangement of the marriage, the betrothal or engagement, the fetching of the bride, the wedding ceremony, and then the marriage feast.

THE ARRANGEMENT

The first step of the ancient Jewish wedding is called the Arrangement or *Shidduchin* in Hebrew. From my all-time favorite musical, *Fiddler on the Roof,* we have a song which captures the essence of how this arrangement process developed in Jewish culture. The words of the song, "Matchmaker, matchmaker make me a match, find me a find, catch me a catch… Matchmaker, matchmaker look through your book and make me a perfect match," describe the arrangement practice in a 20th century Jewish community.

The "Matchmaker" song reflects the first aspect of the Jewish wedding where an arrangement is made. In Fiddler on the Roof, the arrangement is made by a hired matchmaker who is to find the perfect match for Teviah's oldest daughter, Tzeidel. Since Tzeidel is from a poor family, the song goes on to explain her situation "…with no dowry, no money, no family background, be glad you've got a man…" In other words, she should not expect the perfect match. Therefore, the arrangement was the first step, not only in ancient Jewish weddings, but also this custom is kept in some circles to this day.

THE BETROTHAL

The Betrothal, or more simply, engagement, *Eyrusin* in Hebrew, is the next step. This step could last up to a year or more. Traditionally, it is also called the period of sanctification or *Kiddushim* in Hebrew, which means to be set-apart. At this time the groom signed the *Ketubah* or marriage contract. This contract served as a promise and assurance of the groom's love for his bride. During this betrothal period, the bride was being trained and prepared to take on the role of a wife. It also provided an opportunity for her purity to be tested.

The Betrothal ceremony was conducted under a marriage canopy known as a *chuppah*, where both the groom and bride would partake of the blessings over the cup of wine, and recite the betrothal blessings. In fact, the bond of betrothal was as binding as the marriage itself. This covenant could not be broken; to nullify it, they would need to get a divorce.

Before We Begin

THE FETCHING OF THE BRIDE

The Fetching of the Bride was one of the most mysterious and unpredictable customs, but also a very exciting one. What was the groom doing during all this time while the bride continued to anticipate his coming? The groom had many responsibilities. He was the provider and protector of his bride and was busy preparing a suitable home for his beloved. Typically, the groom would build an addition onto his father's home and had to wait for his final approval of the dwelling before he could go to fetch his bride. Since the groom's time of coming was unpredictable, the bride was under constant pressure to always be ready; living in a state of expectancy. In ancient Jewish weddings it was customary for the groom to fetch his bride at nighttime, with torches lighting the way, and with the sound of a sudden shout, proclaiming, "The Groom is coming!"

THE WEDDING CEREMONY

The Wedding Ceremony and Marriage Feast, or *Nissuim* in Hebrew, takes us to the final step in the ancient Jewish wedding that climaxed in the consummation of the marriage. Only a few were invited to the wedding ceremony, whereas many more would be invited to the marriage feast. The day had come and the bride had made herself ready. The father has issued son's permission to get the bride, and all has been prepared by the groom for his beloved bride. While the groom has been preparing a place for his bride, the bride was preparing herself for the groom. Ancient Jewish weddings could last as long as seven days, which signifies the fullness of joy.

In this book we will take a closer look at how each of these wedding steps beautifully point to our relationship with Yeshua, and each one of us as His bride. In chapter one, we will take a look at the first step: the arrangement, what it means to have our heavenly Father as a divine matchmaker, and the value of being chosen.

Sample of Ketubah, a marriage contract (1964)

Blessed be the God and Father of our Lord Yeshua the Messiah, who has blessed us with every spiritual blessing in the heavenly places in Messiah, just as He chose us in Him before the foundation of the world, that we would be holy and blameless before Him.
Ephesians 1:3-4

Chapter 1

You Are His Chosen

A Great Purpose

In school, I always dreaded gym class when the teacher would divide us into two teams for a certain sports activity. First, she would pick two captains, and then the captains would choose individuals one-by-one for their respective teams. I remember thinking and praying, "please don't let me be the last one picked, please don't let me be the last one chosen for a team." It was humiliating waiting there to be chosen to join a team as the group grew smaller and smaller, and then to be the last one chosen was absolutely devastating.

I would have thought, as I grew older and matured as a believer, that these insecurities of not being chosen would have vanished entirely. After all, as a believer in Messiah, a wife, a mother of two sons, and someone who has managed to be in ministry over the years, I should have an adequate perspective of who I am by now. However, as I consider this issue of validation and meaningfulness, I find that often times Stasi Eldredge's poignant description in her book, *Captivating*, gives a sense of my true feelings:

> I know I am not alone in this nagging sense of failure to measure up, a feeling of not being good enough as a woman. Every woman I've ever met feels it—something deeper than just the sense of failing at what she does; an underlying gut feeling of failing at whom she is. I am not enough, and I am too much at the same time. Not pretty enough, not thin enough, not kind enough, not gracious enough, not disciplined enough, too emotional, too needy, too sensitive, too strong, too opinionated, too messy. The result is shame... which haunts us, nipping at our heels, feeding on our deepest fear that we will end up abandoned and alone. After all if we were better women... whatever that means... life wouldn't be so hard...Right?? We wouldn't have so many struggles and sorrows in our hearts. Why is it so hard to create meaningful friendships and sustain them? Why do our days seem so unimportant, filled not with romance and adventure, but with duties and demands? We feel unseen, even by those who are closest to us. We feel unsought...that no one has the passion or the courage to pursue us, to get past our messiness and find the woman deep inside. We feel uncertain of what it means to be a woman.

I think that so many of us feel this way during the various seasons of our lives. Just take a quick look at the magazine covers the next time you are in line at the grocery store checkout. I did just recently, and decided to buy one of the women's magazines. The current issue's headlines revealed that we are constantly trying to figure out how to be accepted, to be thinner, to be younger looking, to be desired, and to be secure in love. I am listing just a few of these headlines:

- Melt away belly bloat (eat this to fit into your skinny jeans!)

- End insomnia and fatigue! (Better sleep secrets)

- Stay young - reverse skin aging with tea! Prevent Alzheimer's with your cell phone! Stop DNA damage with hugs!

- Break free from stress - six ways to silence your inner critic so you can relax and enjoy.

- How to be secure in love - secret ways to make him really care.

A few years ago, I subscribed to one of the monthly health magazines and after several months I began to realize that all the articles were similar in their content, always addressing the issues that we women have. Even the few headline titles that I have listed above are redundant and seem to indicate that women are very concerned about how they look and feel. We want to look younger, be healthier and happier so we will sense our value and feel better about ourselves. We spend lots of time making ourselves desirable and appealing so we can feel attractive. In fact, many of our dysfunctions and addictions flare up when we feel that it's not working and we are not desirable or sought after.

With our Heavenly Father it is completely different. He sees us, knows us, and chooses to love us just as we are, without any cosmetic surgery or weight loss program. This is the one reality that can give us the value that we desperately seek. We need to focus our minds and hearts on the eternal truth of being eternally desired.

Do you ever think and contemplate the fact, that before you were born, God was thinking about you? He knew you in your mother's womb. King David states in Psalm 139:14-17,

> I will give thanks to You, for I am fearfully and wonderfully made; wonderful are Your works, and my soul knows it very well. My frame was not hidden from You, when I was made in secret, and skillfully wrought in the depths of the earth; Your eyes have seen my unformed substance; and in Your book were all written the days that were ordained for me, when as yet there was not one of them. How precious also are Your thoughts to me, O God! How vast is the sum of them!

This passage of Scripture reiterates that your God not only sees you, He also knows you. He knew you before you were born and had a plan for you before He laid the foundations of the world. Knowing this should give us much stability. Think of the opposite idea that somehow you evolved as a random genetic mutation that occurred within your organism's genetic code. This is what Darwin's Theory of Evolution would want us to believe. However, when questioned about the human body and how intricately we are formed, even Darwin admitted:

> To suppose that the eye with all its inimitable contrivances for adjusting the focus to different distances, for admitting different amounts of light, and for the correction of spherical and chromatic aberration, could have been formed by natural selection seems, I freely confess, absurd in the highest degree.

This quote from Darwin sheds light on the fact that there had to be a creator, an intelligent designer of this universe. However, we must realize that our creation is not just the physical body of a person, but also includes the immaterial; the soul and spirit made in our Creator's image. We are not random in our Creator's eyes, not at all, but rather we are specifically created and formed by Him.

This concept of being chosen is so vital to understand and consider that we must stop and think about why God cares so much about His creation. Let's consider why God chose the Jewish people when there wasn't even one Jewish person to choose. Since the same principles apply to a nation as well as an individual, they will be beneficial to strengthen our trust in God's plans for each of us.

JEWISH PEOPLE WERE CHOSEN BY GOD

In the Hebrew Scriptures we see that God specifically chose the Jewish people to demonstrate His love and faithfulness as it states in Deuteronomy 7:6-9. This passage gives details for the reasons God chose the Jewish people.

> Deuteronomy 7:6-9, "For you are a holy people to the LORD your God; the LORD your God has chosen you to be a people for His own possession out of all the peoples who are on the face of the earth. "The LORD did not set His love on you nor choose you because you were more in number than any of the peoples, for you were the fewest of all peoples, but because the LORD loved you and kept the oath which He swore to your forefathers, the LORD brought you out by a mighty hand, and redeemed you from the house of slavery, from the hand of Pharaoh king of Egypt. Know therefore that the LORD your God, He is God, the faithful God, who keeps His covenant and His lovingkindness to a thousandth generation with those who love Him and keep His commandments."

In this section the Hebrew word for "choose" is, *bachar*, and means a desired choice, to prefer, or select. Consider this, did God choose the Jewish people because Israel was the biggest and the greatest nation? Not at all, for according to Deuteronomy 7:7, they were actually the fewest of all people. We see from this portion that God chose to love them and wanted to show that the value of the Jewish people would be based on His love and His ability to keep them as a people.

The prosperity of the Jewish people would never be based on their own strength or resources. Deuteronomy 7:6 also states,

God has chosen you to be a people for His own possession out of all the peoples who are on the face of the earth.

This idea of being "His own possession," uses another Hebrew word, *segulah*, which literally means treasured possession. This word, *segulah*, is reiterated in Deuteronomy 26:18, "And the LORD has today declared you to be His people, a treasured possession (*segulah*), as He promised you, and that you should keep all His commandments."

God declares the people of Israel to be His treasured possession, but what was God's purpose in setting His love upon them? Think of why someone would collect or acquire not only things, but also relationships as treasured possessions. Is it because of love or having ownership that would give a sense of pride and power? Some who have wealth may be collectors of treasures such as rare works of art and would want to add to their collections just to have more assets. If the right opportunity came along, these same collectors could turn around and sell these treasured possessions to the highest bidder. What would you consider your most treasured possession? Perhaps you have something in your jewelry box, or possibly you consider your children your *segulah* or most treasured possession.

We do not serve a capricious God who changes His purpose and plan for His creation. Our Master of the universe always has a master plan, a purpose, and a reason for His choices. God does not need more power, more possessions, or more treasures. We must not forget the underlying characteristic in His choosing that is summed up in God's covenant love. God chose to set His love on the nation of Israel to show even greater love. He called Abram and established the Abrahamic covenant and this is what God stated to Abram before there was a Jewish nation:

> Genesis 12:1-3, "Now the LORD said to Abram, Go forth from your country, And from your relatives And from your father's house, To the land which I will show you; And I will make you a great nation, And I will bless you, And make your name great; And so you will be a blessing; And I will bless those who bless you, And the one who curses you I will curse. And in you all the families of the earth will be blessed."

We see that the purpose of Israel to become a nation is so that God would bless them and in turn they would be a vessel of blessing to all the families of the earth. Through Abraham's seed, Messiah Yeshua would bring the ultimate redemption and blessing to the world.

FROM ERRORS TO TREASURES

The history of Israel is fraught with twists and turns as they rebel against God's plans and purposes. God is always faithful to provide what is needed to keep His master plan in motion. He uses His treasured possession to be a blessing to the world. Throughout Israel's history we see God's plan for individuals such as Moses, who was chosen to redeem the children of Israel out of slavery in Egypt. Initially, Moses found a number of excuses for not wanting to embrace this call of God. Perhaps he felt that God was forty years too late. We read in Exodus 2:11-13 that Moses had tried to defend his Jewish brethren, but was rejected by them and then escaped from Pharaoh.

When God's call came at the burning bush in the desert, Moses had already spent another forty years herding his father-in-law's flocks being a shepherd. He probably felt like a failure in a dead end job and didn't see himself as the heroic deliverer of the Jewish people. God did not make a mistake in calling Moses. He knew him intimately and was always preparing His servant throughout his life. God's timing is always perfect and God did not waste the experiences of Moses, but rather used all that he had been through as preparation to lead Israel from bondage. Think of the first forty years in Egypt and how he received the best education available in the known world. Then as a shepherd of sheep, for another forty years he developed the patience and love that he would need to become a shepherd of a wayward nation.

Consider for a moment your own life. Maybe you feel as though somehow God's plan for you has not turned out as you had hoped. Do not despair, God will not waste any of the suffering, the heartaches, the victories, the years supporting your husband, raising your children and loving your grandchildren. We have a Redeemer who will restore, renew, and revive us as we turn everything over to His capable hands. He wants to use it all to bring Him glory. God calls you and me His treasured possession or *segulah*. The following verses precisely illustrate this tender, loving thought:

> 1 Peter 2:9, "But you are a chosen race, a royal priesthood, a holy nation, a people for God's own possession, that you may proclaim the excellencies of Him who has called you out of darkness into His marvelous light."

> Titus 2:14, "who gave Himself for us, that He might redeem us from every lawless deed and purify for Himself a people for His own possession, zealous for good deeds."

God wanted His people to be delivered from bondage for a purpose, to bring Him honor through worship and service. God reveals to Moses the reason for their freedom,

> Exodus 3:12, "Certainly I will be with you, and this shall be the sign to you that it is I who have sent you: when you have brought the people out of Egypt, you shall worship God at this mountain"

The word "sign", *ot* in Hebrew, means a witness or miraculous sign. It indicates that freedom from slavery would not be a chance to get out of Egypt and party day and night, but rather a time to worship the God of Israel. It would be a testimony to the surrounding nations that Israel belonged to *El Shaddai*, God Almighty, through worshiping Him. God's choosing of Israel was to show what it looked like to belong to Him. Even in the meaning of the word "worship", *avad* in Hebrew, there is a broader sense of what God desires from Israel.

From the Hebrew *avad* we have *avodah*, which means both worshipper and servant. In our relationship with God, He desires for us to both worship Him and serve Him with our whole heart, strength, and mind. This would be the sign (*ot*), the witness, and the testimony to the nations who knew only of idols and gods of their own making.

CHOSEN FOR A PURPOSE

Ephesians 1:3-6, "Blessed be the God and Father of our Lord Yeshua the Messiah, who has blessed us with every spiritual blessing in the heavenly places in Messiah, just as He chose us in Him before the foundation of the world, that we should be holy and blameless before Him. In love He predestined us to adoption as sons through Yeshua the Messiah to Himself, according to the kind intention of His will, to the praise of the glory of His grace, which He freely bestowed on us in the Beloved.

In this New Covenant portion we see that the Greek word for "choose" is *eklego*. The word, *eklego*, gives the same meaning as its Hebrew counterpart because it carries the idea that God selects us and picks us out; this is not a haphazard choice, but rather this is a choice with purpose and love.

Ephesians 1:4 reiterates that He chose you before the foundation of the world. Along with His choosing, we also have a reason for His choice, which says that we are to reflect His character, to be holy and blameless, and to be His children showing what it means to belong to God. We are to display to the world the character of a holy and loving God.

HE CHOSE YOU TO BLESS YOU

In the Scriptures, God promised Israel material blessings as a reward for their obedience.

Deuteronomy 28:1-4, "Now it shall be, if you will diligently obey the LORD your God, being careful to do all His commandments which I command you today, the LORD your God will set you high above all the nations of the earth. All these blessings shall come upon you and overtake you, if you will obey the LORD your God: "Blessed shall you be in the city, and blessed shall you be in the country. Blessed shall be the offspring of your body and the produce of your ground and the offspring of your beasts, the increase of your herd and the young of your flock."

This portion speaks of wonderful conditional blessings. In other words, if you obey me, then you will be blessed. In the case of Deuteronomy 28, these blessings have to do with physical and material prosperity. However, Paul's blessing in Ephesians 1:3-6 goes well beyond this portion in Deuteronomy:

> Blessed be the God and Father of our Lord Yeshua the Messiah, who has blessed us with every spiritual blessing in the heavenly places in Messiah. (Ephesians 1:3)

God promises to supply all of our needs according to His riches in glory by Messiah Yeshua. Furthermore, Paul states in Philippians 4:19 that it is according to, or in proportion to, His riches in the heavenly places.

> Philippians 4:19, "And my God will meet all your needs according to his glorious riches in Messiah Yeshua."

In other words, all the riches that God possesses, He is willing to provide to benefit you. We are never without resources when we are in Messiah. His resources are limitless, His riches are untraceable, and therefore your benefits in Yeshua are inexhaustible.

Notice that Philippians 4:19 says that God will give us all of our needs. We may think we know what we need and what we want. However, God who has wonderfully woven us in our mother's womb has placed those needs in us. He knows exactly what we need. God does not desire that we go around feeling unappreciated, unloved, and insecure, but just the opposite. These are the very needs that should drive us to His throne and to a deeper walk with Him. God delights in our fellowship and He placed in us the need for a relationship with Him and others.

God does not promise to shield us from problems, difficulties, or pain, but He promises to bring us through. He promises every blessing to be poured out into our lives through His Spirit. He will give us everything we need to bring us through each situation in life. He desires for us to have an abundant spiritual life lived out to the fullest, and overflowing (John 10:10).

Elizabeth Elliot gives us a great perspective on God's promise to sustain us no matter what we are going through:

> Nothing can reach us, from any source on earth or hell, no matter how evil, which God cannot turn to his own redemptive purpose. Let us be glad that the way is not a game of chance, a mere roll of dice which determines our fortune or calamity—it is a way appointed, and it is appointed for God's eternal glory and our final good.

How can we know that He has a plan for us individually and for the Body of Messiah? How can we trace His work in our lives? Sometimes it seems like our lives are a moving target without any rhyme or reason.

The Scriptures assure us that our times are in His hands (Psalm 31:15); one of the ways to understand God's plan and commitment to us is through the ancient Jewish wedding customs. There is a progression that is seen throughout these customs that will give us confidence in the plans of our Heavenly Matchmaker.

HE CHOSE YOU AS HIS BRIDE

You might be familiar with the phrase, "I'm always a bridesmaid, never a bride," which usually is expressed with disappointment and regret. What is the difference between being a bridesmaid and bride? After all, a bridesmaid gets to wear a beautiful dress, has a lovely bouquet of flowers, and is sometimes matched up with a handsome groomsman. In contrast, the bride is chosen specifically by her groom to be his wife and this is the point of the celebration.

Do you remember what it was like to be proposed to? Can you relive that feeling of being totally accepted and loved at that very moment? As we parallel the traditional Jewish wedding with what our God has done, we will see that in the mind of God, He has it all planned out for you and your Groom from the beginning through eternity. God already chose you and your Heavenly Father is the ultimate wedding planner.

THE GREATEST WEDDING PLANNER

As noted before, the first step in the Jewish wedding is called the arrangement (or *shiddukhin*). This custom is still observed in orthodox Jewish homes today. This arrangement (*shiddukhin*) is described in Genesis 24:1-4 where Abraham desires to provide a bride for his son Isaac. Abraham sends his chief servant to go and find a wife for his son which turned out to be beautiful Rebekah.

If we take a closer look at Ephesians 1:3-4, we discover that an essential part of the spiritual blessing in our Messiah is the fact that the Father chose you to be Messiah's bride even before the foundation of the world. Your heavenly Father made your marriage arrangement with you in His mind.

> Ephesians 1:3-4, "Blessed be the God and Father of our Lord Yeshua the Messiah, who has blessed us with every spiritual blessing in the heavenly places in Messiah, just as He chose us in Him before the foundation of the world, that we should be holy and blameless before Him."

In the section of this Scripture we find the doctrine of election that can be both confusing and confounding. If we understand that Messiah said the same thing to His disciples in John 15:16, it gives us a broader perspective. Messiah tells His disciples:

> John 15:16, "You did not choose Me, but I chose you, and appointed you, that you should go and bear fruit, and that your fruit should remain, that whatever you ask of the Father in My name, He may give to you."

Messiah clearly states that us choosing Him and being led to salvation always begins with God. For He says: "you did not choose Me, but I chose you." In fact, initially we were completely unable to choose God. Isaiah 53:6 describes it this way, "All we like sheep have gone astray, each of us has turned to his own way."

The Scriptures teach us that God is always seeking you and me. Even before He created the universe, it was evident that our restoration back to God would be wholly dependent on His love and grace, not on any works we could do. Our responsibility is to respond to God's grace by our own free will. God did not make you a robot so that you would have to love Him. God never forces His love upon us, but desires that we respond to His love by depending on His grace.

HIS KIND INTENTION TOWARD YOU

This mystery of Divine sovereignty and human responsibility will never be completely understood in this life, but both are Biblical and essential for us as we mature as His bride. The declaration of Messiah choosing His disciples is seen in the intimate setting of the Passover meal. His instructions for us are just as applicable today as for those who followed Him then. In John 15:13-17 it states,

> Greater love has no one than this that one lay down his life for his friends. You are My friends if you do what I command you. No longer do I call you slaves, for the slave does not know what his master is doing; but I have called you friends, for all things that I have heard from My Father I have made known to you. You did not choose Me, but I chose you, and appointed you, that you should go and bear fruit, and that your fruit should remain, that whatever you ask of the Father in My name, He may give to you. This I command you, that you love one another.

Your Groom will not force His love on you. He desires you and has chosen you, but you must, by your own free will, say "Yes, I desire this relationship." Each of us must say to the Lord: "Yes, I choose to follow You. I want to be Your bride." Yet we live in a sin sick society where some seem to be out to get something and use the other person for their own advantage. Even immature believers may be looking for a way to leverage their relationships. When I consider the synonyms for leverage, which are weight, control, influence, power and force, it becomes easier to understand why we have difficulty in trusting our groom. The Word of God addresses this tendency to mistrust and misconstrue the motives of our Groom. In Ephesians 1:5 it states,

> "He predestined us to adoption as sons through Yeshua the Messiah to Himself, according to the kind intention of His will."

When we read this phrase, "the kind intention of His will," it should immediately engender confidence and trust in the One who is determining the plans for our lives. Other versions translate this phrase, "the good pleasure of His will" (KJV) and "in accordance with His pleasure and will" (NIV).

Our Groom does not desire to leverage His relationship with us for harm or evil. There is no hidden agenda with our Messiah. He desires to reveal the mystery of His love and purpose to us so that we would know without a doubt that He always has our best interest in His heart.

Why is it so difficult for us to say yes to Yeshua, and let Him be the Lord of our present and future? Perhaps, we are acting according to the flesh and not allowing the Holy Spirit to have dominion over our thoughts and desires. Consequently, we will act in rebellion, mistrust, selfishness and insist to have it our own way. Nonetheless, Scriptures teach us that even when we are wayward, His love will never fail and His plan will not change. For example, God speaks through His prophet to His people in Jeremiah 29:11,

> "For I know the plans that I have for you, declares the LORD, plans for welfare and not for calamity to give you a future and a hope."

This verse shows that while Israel was still in exile, God assured them that He had plans for them. The word "plan" in Hebrew also means design, thoughts, or intention. This verse also indicates that His plans are to give them a future, which carries the idea of posterity. Likewise His purposes for us today are for *shalom* (peace), fulfillment and contentment, and not for evil or misery. Your Groom's kind intention toward you is only for your good and He proved it by paying the bride price.

THE BRIDE PRICE

According to the Jewish marriage customs, part of the arrangement, or *shiddukhin*, is the payment by the father of the bride price (*mohar*). The payment could occur when the couple is very young, or it might not happen until they meet on their wedding day.

For us, as believers in Messiah, this payment of the bride price is of vital significance. Your bride price has been completely covered by Your heavenly Father, who put His love for you in a contract that reflects His covenant love.

When Messiah was celebrating Passover with His disciples, just before He gave His life as the Passover Lamb, He took the third cup of redemption after the Passover meal and said, "This cup which is poured out for you is the new covenant in My blood" (Luke 22:20). This New Covenant is our marriage contract, (*Ketubah*), which was given in Messiah's blood. A *Ketubah,* which is a legal binding document, is still used in Jewish marriages today. Messiah sealed and legalized His *Ketubah* with us similarly to the relationships between husbands and wives. In Ephesians 5 Paul reiterates, "this mystery is great; but I am speaking with reference to Messiah and the congregation." Messiah, our Groom, died on behalf of His bride to pay the bride price.

> Ephesians 5:24-27, "Just as the Body of Messiah submits to the Messiah, so also wives should submit to their husbands in everything. As for husbands, love your wives, just as the Messiah loved the Body of Messiah, indeed, gave himself up on its behalf, that He might sanctify her, having cleansed her by the washing of water with the word, that He might present to Himself the Congregation in all her glory, having no spot or wrinkle or any such thing; but that she should be holy and blameless."

Each time I read how Messiah wants to present me in all my glory, "having no spot or wrinkle or any such thing" I am reminded that this is the best beauty secret of the ages. I don't need to find the fountain of youth to be a beautiful bride forever. However, I must let the words of my Groom make me pure in order to be transformed into His image to reflect His beauty and holiness.

As Messiah's Bride you are seen, you are sought after, and you can be secure in His Love. Messiah fulfills the deepest needs in our hearts as we desire romance, to be pursued, to be needed, to be valued in this great adventure called life, and to have our inner beauty unveiled.

The headlines from women's magazines reflect our inner desires, just as some of the lines from those classic romantic movies. They illustrate the deep hunger we have in our hearts to be pursued, to be valued, and to be loved:

- In *The Last of the Mohicans*, Nathaniel says to Cora, "I will find you, no matter how long it takes, no matter how far…I will find you."

- In *Show me the Money*, Jerry McGuire, when he finally realizes he is in love, goes back to his wife and declares passionately, "You complete me…"

- In *Sense and Sensibility*, when Edward finally returns to proclaim his love for Elinor, "Then…you're not married?" Elinor says. "No," replies Edward, "my heart is and always will be yours."

Your Groom, Yeshua the Messiah, declares the same to you. His heart will always be yours. He chose you, He pursues you, He desires you, and He loves you. You are His top priority. Consequently, if we focus on our Groom, Messiah, we can state with confidence every day, "I am chosen, I am loved and I am His Bride forever."

Your true worth and significance is found in your Creator, through Yeshua, your Groom, and it's sealed by the Holy

Spirit. After the choosing process or the arrangement, your relationship has just begun and there is vital work to do while you're waiting for your Groom to return. In the next chapter we will discuss what to do while we are waiting for our Groom, Yeshua.

QUESTIONS AND REFLECTIONS:

1. Read Psalm 139:14-17 and spend time thanking the Lord for how He created you.

2. How does the concept of God choosing you impact your life each day? Consider Ephesians 1:3-6 and John 15:16.

3. Consider that Yeshua your Groom paid the Bride price for you and think of what things or people in your life would hinder you from realizing how special you are to God.

4. Where is your true significance found in this life?

Sanctify Messiah as Lord in your hearts, always being ready to make a defense to everyone who asks you to give an account for the hope that is in you, yet with gentleness and reverence.
1 Peter 3:15

Chapter 2

While We Are Waiting

Everything You Do Matters to God

*I*magine an ideal wedding. A beautiful ceremony has been conducted under the lovely *Chuppah* (wedding canopy), sacred vows exchanged, and Hebrew blessings uttered. The covenant of marriage has been articulated, and the *Ketubah* has been signed. All is in perfect harmony. It seemed that everyone joined in the celebration at the reception. While dancing the traditional *Horah*, there was much rejoicing as the bride and groom were hoisted into the air on chairs. Positive responses from the guests were heard as the bride and groom were leaving, "Wow what a marvelous time of joy and celebration!" "Shlomo and Esther look perfect together! Surely they will live happily ever after."

But what if, as the limousine drives away amid the shouts of *Mazel Tov* and well wishes, Esther begins to move away from her groom to the other side of the car window? Suddenly, she announces in a slightly irritated voice, "Shlomo, I'm really tired, please take me home." And Shlomo replies in astonishment, "Home? But darling, you know our home won't be ready for a few more weeks. We're going on our honeymoon now. I can't take you home. The heat and the water aren't even connected yet."

"Oh, I don't mean to your home, I mean to my home, take me back to my mother. Look Shlomo, now that we are married, I'll try to see you once a week if it's convenient, but I'm going back to my old way of life. Of course I love you, Shlomo. After all I've accepted you as my husband, haven't I? Don't think that I am going to change the way I live. Unless of course, I get sick, or if I need more money, or if something comes up that I can't handle, then I'll call you right away. I'll expect you to take care of things because you are my husband, and after all, we signed the *Ketubah* together. In the meantime, thank you for loving me, thank you for making me yours, but hands off my life."

This may sound like a ludicrous or even absurd scene. It wouldn't be a marriage at all. No intimacy, no sense of commitment from the bride, only from the groom. What kind of a relationship would this be?

However as ludicrous as this may seem, sometimes our commitment to Yeshua can resemble this illustration.

In the first chapter we considered the initial step in the Jewish wedding, The Arrangement, or *shiddukin*, where our heavenly matchmaker "made us a match." He chose and demonstrated His love for us by providing the perfect Groom.

In response, we have given our hearts to Him and now the second phase can begin. After the arrangement is finalized the next step is the betrothal or the engagement period. According to Jewish wedding customs, to be betrothed means that you are married, even though the physical consummation will take place at a later time.

THE BETROTHAL PERIOD

Let's take a deeper look at the second step in the ancient Jewish wedding called, "Betrothal," or *Eyrusin* in Hebrew. At this betrothal, the groom signs the *Ketubah* or marriage contract which serves as a promise and assurance of the groom's love for his bride.

The betrothal step is conducted under the wedding canopy called a *"chuppah,"* where the groom and bride partake of a cup of wine and recite the betrothal blessings. This signifies that the bond of betrothal or engagement is as good as marriage. The covenant cannot be broken.

Consider that the Upper Room where Yeshua and His disciples celebrated Passover was a Divine *Chuppah*. In this most intimate setting, Yeshua lifted up the cup of wine and said these words, "This cup which is poured out for you is the new covenant in My blood" (Luke 22:20). This signifies that the Bride price is paid for by His blood, and the *Ketubah*, or New Covenant, is sealed.

The Scriptures teach us that, in general, there could be no covenant made without the shedding of blood. Our Groom, Yeshua, invites you and me into the most intimate relationship based on a covenant that cannot be broken because it is sealed by His own blood.

To understand how serious the idea of engagement was we have the example in the Gospels of when Joseph was betrothed to Miriam. After he found out she was with child, Joseph was going to divorce her privately until an angel appeared to Joseph and explained the situation.

Consider what Miriam did when she was waiting for Joseph to come for her. She may not have understood how everything would work out, but she trusted God and she trusted her groom. How encouraged she must have been when the angel interceded on her behalf with the message to her, "…and you will bear a Son; and you shall call His name Yeshua, for it is He who will save His people from their sins" (Luke 1:31-32). Just as Miriam had to wait until Joseph prepared a home for her, we too must wait while Yeshua prepares a home for us. In the case of Miriam and Joseph, the unexplained mystery almost interrupted their betrothal bond, yet the angel came at just the right time to intercede.

A TIME TO PREPARE

What a privilege Miriam had, not only to wait, but also to prepare her heart for her groom. Traditionally this betrothal period is also known as the period of sanctification or *Kiddushin*, which means, to be set-apart to holiness. This is the period of time when the bride is being trained and prepared to take on the role of a wife. The betrothal provides an opportunity for her purity to be tested.

Kiddush is based on the Hebrew word *kadosh*, (holy), and it means to sanctify or set apart. Our *Ketubah*, the New Covenant, takes this concept to a deeper level in 1 Peter 3:15.

> "But sanctify Messiah as Lord in your hearts, always being ready to make a defense to everyone who asks you to give an account for the hope that is in you, yet with gentleness and reverence."

In other words, we are to honor, make holy, or sanctify the name of Messiah in our hearts during this time of engagement as we are waiting for Him to return. It is vital to ask ourselves questions that reveal our inner heart attitude. As I wait, am I keeping myself pure, continually believing in the kind intentions of my beloved? Do I trust that when he is finished preparing a home and all is ready, He will return? Do I sometimes doubt his love and fidelity for me? The best gift that I can give my Beloved is a heart fully yielded to Him. There is nothing greater that we can offer Yeshua than our undivided life, wholly submitted to His Word.

Our Groom told us that He is preparing a place for us and He will come to get us when all is ready, but what are we to be doing while we wait? It is so essential for us to understand that while we wait, everything we do each day matters to God. Your motives, your behavior, and your service to the Lord are important to Him. As you sanctify Messiah as Lord in your heart and bring honor to His name, these righteous acts will be displayed at your ultimate wedding celebration when Your Groom returns for you.

Revelation 19:8 explains it this way, "It was given to her to clothe herself in fine linen, bright and clean; for the fine linen is the righteous acts of the saints." Notice the description of the clothing of the bride. It is fine linen which is reflecting the most beautiful and exquisite of all clothes. The verse explains that this fine linen clothing is made up of the righteous deeds of the bride while on earth. This external clothing is a result of being filled with the Holy Spirit. The prophet Isaiah tells us that all the deeds done in the power of our flesh are like filthy garments before the Lord.

> Isaiah 64:6, "For all of us have become like one who is unclean, and all of our righteous deeds are like a filthy garment..."

However, in stark contrast, those works that we have accomplished in the power of God's Spirit reflect the very character of God in our lives. His fruit of love, joy, peace, patience, kindness, and goodness will bring honor to God. If you say that you trust in Yeshua but do not honor Him, then you are far from God and you are bringing dishonor to His name. This is why we need to be concerned about our daily activities because they will be seen in these white linen garments. Everything we do matters to God.

YOU ARE CREATED FOR GOOD WORKS

Remember how Esther acted toward her new groom Shlomo? Many times we may dishonor the Name of our Groom by treating Him merely as our emergency go-to person. God expects us to live in such a way that reflects the fact that we are his workmanship. Paul explains in Ephesians 2:8-9,

"For by grace you have been saved through faith; and that not of yourselves, it is the gift of God; not as a result of works, that no one should boast."

Here we see that God chose us, and by faith in His provision we come into this intimate relationship with Yeshua, our Groom. Paul goes on to explain that we have work to do on our Groom's behalf.

Ephesians 2:10, "For we are His workmanship, created in Messiah Yeshua for good works, which God prepared beforehand, that we would walk in them."

During this betrothal period we are preparing, and even today, this time of preparation is described in different cultures. The French term, *trousseau*, has to do with the preparation a bride makes for her marriage. It is usually a collection of the clothes and linen, especially items such as nightgowns, blankets, and sheets, which she has collected during the period of her engagement.

When I was growing up I remember my mother showing me a beautiful cedar chest. She called it a "hope chest". Since my sister was older and expected to marry first she would inherit this hope chest on her wedding day. This chest contained hand embroidered lacey pillow cases and sheets as well as beautiful quilts. These items were made with love and with the expectation that this hope chest would show how much the bride loved and appreciated her new husband.

As we parallel this idea to our spiritual walk we need to ask the question: What kind of spiritual hope chest am I building during this betrothal period?

THE WISE BUILDER

In 1 Corinthians 3:9-16 Paul exhorts the congregation at Corinth to be wise in how they are building their lives. We can apply this example as we think of how we are building our trousseau and consider the issue of what we are hoping for each day.

> "For we are God's fellow workers; you are God's field, God's building. According to the grace of God which was given to me, as a wise master builder I laid a foundation, and another is building upon it. But let each man be careful how he builds upon it. For no man can lay a foundation other than the one which is laid, which is Yeshua the Messiah. Now if any man builds upon the foundation with gold, silver, precious stones, wood, hay, straw, each man's work will become evident; for the day will show it, because it is to be revealed with fire; and the fire itself will test the quality of each man's work. If any man's work which he has built upon it remains, he shall receive a reward. If any man's work is burned up, he shall suffer loss; but he himself shall be saved, yet so as through fire. Do you not know that you are a temple of God, and that the Spirit of God dwells in you?"

Are you building your life on the foundation of your Groom's love and His promise to return for you? Paul is explaining that just as a master builder understood the significance of the building's foundation, so each believer in the body of Messiah must lay the same foundation, which is building upon the Lord. If you are not building according to God's grace in you and with the goal of lifting up Yeshua, then your works will not stand on that day of testing. The testing of the quality of our work will be evident when we stand before His purifying fire. As His bride, each of us will give an account for how we use our time, our God given gifts, and resources. The value and quality of the intentions of your heart reflect your daily activities.

One day you will stand before Him. Your husband will not be with you, your children will not be with you, and your trusted friend will not be there either. It will be just you and Yeshua. As you stand before Him, your deeds will go through the fires of testing to see who and what you were trusting in. All that was accomplished by grace through faith will be as gold, silver, and precious stones.

On the other hand, the wood, hay, and straw represent the motives and conduct that come as a result of trusting in something other than the foundation that Messiah has laid. These truths should not frighten us but rather inspire us to draw close to Yeshua each day in worship and study of His word. I want to receive rewards that will stand the test of His purifying fire so that I can lay them at the feet of my Messiah in utter thankfulness for His saving love.

This purity is tested as we live out our relationship with Yeshua. The Scriptures are clear about God's purpose for us. 1 Thessalonians 4:3-4 says,

> "For this is the will of God, your sanctification; that is, that you abstain from sexual immorality; that each of you know how to possess his own vessel in sanctification *(kiddushin)* and honor."

HOLY TO THE LORD

The aspect of God's will that is being emphasized is for each person's sanctification or holiness. Paul puts it this way in I Thessalonians 3:13, "so that He may establish your hearts without blame in holiness before our God and Father at the coming of our Lord Yeshua with all His saints."

This holiness carries the idea of being set apart for, or dedicated to God based on the atonement of Messiah. It does not mean that each of us have attained to holiness or sanctification but that we are in the process of being made holy, being conformed to the image of Messiah, and growing to be like God in our character and conduct. This sanctification is seen in the purity of our lives. God's desire is for each of us to grow in holiness; this is His will for us. In 2 Corinthians 11:2-3 Paul says to the Corinthian believer,

> "For I am jealous (*zeloo*) for you with a godly jealousy; for I betrothed you to one husband, so that to Messiah I might present you as a pure virgin. But I am afraid that, as the serpent deceived Eve by his craftiness, your minds should be led astray from the simplicity and purity of devotion to Messiah."

The word "pure" in Greek and in Hebrew means to be free from ceremonial defilement, holy, sacred, free from sin, or innocent. King David prayed that God would create in him a pure heart, *lev tahor*, in Hebrew. A heart that is spotless, stainless, and free from moral fault or guilt, and unmixed with any other matter. This is not about being outwardly clean, like using Ivory soap that is 99.99% pure, but as the Scriptures say, "Though your sins are as scarlet, they shall be white as snow" (Isaiah 1:18).

God cleanses us and we are like a virgin before Him. Just as any man would be jealous if his wife went after other man, so Messiah is jealous for you. He wants you to be pure and faithful to Him alone and not to prostitute yourself to the gods of this world. You are His pure virgin. He has cleansed you and bought you with His blood. We can sometimes be very creative in our desire and ability to go after other things that defile us and take us away from putting Yeshua first.

EVE'S MISTAKE

Eve was led astray by the craftiness of the evil one. Paul writes,

> "Lest your minds should be led astray from the simplicity and purity of devotion to Messiah" (2 Corinthians 11:3).

Eve's curiosity and her insatiable desire to be like God led her to listen to Satan, the father of lies. The word "mind" can also be translated purpose or thought. The seeds of doubt that the serpent sowed refocused Eve's thoughts away from the pure relationship she had with her Creator. Her deception began as she listened to the serpent and began to think, "Maybe God has not given me everything that I need; maybe God is holding back on me." Throughout the chapter, Paul warns the Corinthians not to be taken in by false teachers. As he defends his position and authority as a true apostle, he warns them.

> 2 Corinthians 11:13-14, "For such men are false apostles, deceitful workers, disguising themselves as apostles of Messiah. No wonder, for even Satan disguises himself as an angel of light."

HOW YOU THINK MATTERS

Is your thought life leading you towards purity or defilement? You might be saying in your heart, "What I think is my business! It's not hurting anyone, and besides, I'm the only one who is aware of it!" Or you might say, "I can think about another man. It's nothing more than an innocent flirtation." In this world of Facebook, Twitter, and Pinterest, we need to be aware that sometimes our thoughts become public for the whole world to read. Your Groom sees your heart and knows your thoughts and knows what you need.

However, it is difficult to wait and live a pure life in such a defiled world. We may focus on the many needs of our lives. I need a man to change my tires and fix my leaky roof; I need a date for Saturday night; I need to be supported in the way I have become accustomed. These felt needs are a mere shadow of the deep longings of the heart to be loved and accepted. Ladies, all your needs can be met in your Eternal King and Groom. He is the hero you have been waiting for.

In Paul's day when he was writing to the congregation in Corinth, the society they lived in was as decadent as our anti-god culture today. In the city of Corinth more than one thousand women served as priestesses and prostitutes in the Temple of Aphrodite. After the gospel penetrated this licentious city, Paul wrote to the Corinthian believers, outlining a spectrum of immoral activities that characterized these people before they came to faith in Messiah. Paul is stirring up the believers in Corinth by reminding them of what Messiah has accomplished in them.

1 Corinthians 6: 9-11, "Or do you not know that the unrighteous shall not inherit the kingdom of God? Do not be deceived; neither fornicators, nor idolaters, nor adulterers, nor effeminate, nor homosexuals, nor thieves, nor the covetous, nor drunkards, nor revilers, nor swindlers, shall inherit the kingdom of God. And such were some of you; but you were washed, but you were sanctified, but you were justified in the name of the Lord Yeshua the Messiah, and in the Spirit of our God."

You see, the fact of the matter is, none of us are good enough. We all fit in this list. I covet. I want what others have and am envious. I am an idolater when I put other things as idols above my love for Yeshua. I cheat, and the list goes on for me and for each of you, but as we read, "but you were washed, but you were sanctified, but you were justified in the name of the Lord Yeshua the Messiah, and in the Spirit of our God." Hallelujah!

THE CLEANSING

According to Jewish customs, before the wedding ceremony the bride had to go through the cleansing by way of *Mikvah*, or ritual bath. We will appear before the *Bema* (judgement) seat of Messiah and go through the purification process that will test our lives. Only those deeds that survive the purifying fire will be left and the rest will be burned up.

The purpose of this purifying fire is not for judging sin because Messiah took all of our judgment upon Him. This is a time to evaluate the motives, behavior, and service done for Messiah day by day. He desires to give us rewards for the deeds done in faith to honor Yeshua and to bring honor to His name, the name which is above every name.

Our white linen clothing will reflect the deeds that are done to bring Him honor and glory while we wait. During this betrothal period, may we encourage and challenge one another to keep ourselves pure, to sanctify Messiah as Lord in our hearts, and build our "hope chest" upon the foundation of Yeshua, our Groom.

It's not about a race to do a bunch of good works, but your heart commitment to trust your Groom. Bring honor to His name in whatever you do while you wait for Him to return.

QUESTIONS AND REFLECTIONS:

1. Consider the account of Miriam when she was told by the angel Gabriel that she would be the mother of the Messiah, Luke 1:26-56. How was Miriam's response in verse 38 the key for her during this engagement period to Joseph?

2. Reflect on your life since you became a believer in Yeshua as your Savior. How are you preparing to spend eternity with your Groom?

3. What does 1 Peter 3:15 mean to you and how do you explain the hope that is in you?

4. Describe in your own words how Eve was led astray and the application for your life today. (2 Corinthians 11:3)

For the Lord Himself will descend from heaven with a shout, with the voice of the archangel and with the trumpet of God, and the dead in Messiah will rise first. Then we who are alive and remain will be caught up together with them in the clouds to meet the Lord in the air, and so we shall always be with the Lord.
1 Thessalonians 4:16-17

Chapter 3

Living In Readiness

The Fetching of the Bride

We have come to the third step in the wedding process which is both mysterious and unpredictable. It is a period of waiting that requires patience. Even as I studied the material I was convicted regarding my lack of eagerness and patience when it came to this third stage called, *The Fetching of the Bride*.

Why is it so difficult to be patient? Generally, we resent postponements and delays of scheduled events because we live in a society that is accustomed to immediate gratification. None of us have enough love and patience for the next phase of the Jewish wedding. This is a time that will test the forbearance of even the most committed bride. We always have a choice to trust and be patient or we can choose not to trust and be impatient. As we learn from the life of the newly appointed King of Israel, being impatient and not trusting God's timing can have costly consequences. In fact, Saul learned the hard way that it could cost him his kingdom.

The narrative of this account is found in 1 Samuel 13:7-8. We find Saul waiting in Gilgal for the prophet Samuel to come and bless the impending battle with the fierce Philistines. As Saul was waiting for Samuel to arrive, "the people were scattering from him." Impatient Saul decided to take matters into his own hands and do something that was strictly forbidden by God.

> 1 Samuel 13:9-14, "So Saul said, 'Bring to me the burnt offering and the peace offerings. And he offered the burnt offering. As soon as he finished offering the burnt offering, behold, Samuel came; and Saul went out to meet him and to greet him. But Samuel said, "What have you done?" And Saul said, "Because I saw that the people were scattering from me, and that you did not come within the appointed days, and that the Philistines were assembling at Michmash, therefore I said, 'Now the Philistines will come down against me at Gilgal, and I have not asked the favor of the LORD.' So I forced myself and offered the burnt offering." Samuel said to Saul, "You have acted foolishly; you have not kept the commandment of the LORD your God, which He commanded you, for now the LORD would have established your kingdom over Israel forever. But now your kingdom shall not endure. The LORD has sought out for Himself a man after His own heart, and the LORD has appointed him as ruler

over His people, because you have not kept what the LORD commanded you.'"

Saul's impatience caused him to disregard and disobey the clear word of God. Samuel was the one to offer the sacrifice and bring the blessing of the battle upon the children of Israel. If only Saul had trusted God and waited just a little longer. His impatience cost him his Kingdom. He disregarded the words of the Lord and his prophet Samuel by taking matters into his own hands.

GOD'S SLOWNESS EQUATES HIS KINDNESS

Today we live in an impatient society just as in the days of the apostles. Listen to what Peter says to those who are mocking the Lord and ignoring His warnings to trust in Messiah.

> 2 Peter 3:3-4, "Know this first of all, that in the last days mockers will come with their mocking, following after their own lusts, and saying, "Where is the promise of His coming? For ever since the fathers fell asleep, all continues just as it was from the beginning of creation."

> 2 Peter 3:8-9, "But do not let this one fact escape your notice, beloved, that with the Lord one day is as a thousand years, and a thousand years as one day. The Lord is not slow about His promise, as some count slowness, but is patient toward you, not wishing for any to perish but for all to come to repentance."

What we consider to be the tarrying of His return is in fact the very demonstration of His compassion toward those who reject Him. Moreover, how great is His patient love toward His chosen bride? Instead of considering the groom being slow to return we should see this time as a gift to prepare for our groom's arrival. This particular stage has both an element of surprise and mystery. This eager anticipation for His return has an intrinsic value to be ready at any moment since the exact timing of the groom's return is not known.

REDEMPTION OF THE SOUL AND BODY

At the very first Passover when God was redeeming the children of Israel from bondage they had to be ready to leave at a moment's notice. They were to prepare the meal by slaying the lamb and placing the blood on the door. How did they eat the first Passover meal with lamb, bitter herbs, and *matzah*? The Scriptures explain that they were to partake of this meal with their sandals still on their feet, their long robes fastened about them to be able to travel, and a staff in their hand. As they heeded the instructions of Moses, it was evident that they had to be ready to leave at any moment. They were to anticipate their release from bondage with readiness and preparedness. This is our job, as well as we wait for our groom. At any time our Groom could return and He expects us to be ready to leave.

Instead of growing anxious or doubtful, the wise bride knows in her heart that because of her groom's great love for her, when all the preparations are finished and the time is right, he will return at just the right moment. She knows that she is desired by her beloved. Every day she must keep in the forefront of her thinking that this present betrothal period is her opportunity to make herself ready to meet her groom.

AUSPICIOUS PREPARATIONS

While the bride is making herself ready, what is the groom doing? The groom is also getting ready; he is preparing a place for his bride. During this betrothal time the groom has many responsibilities. As the provider and protector of his bride, he has to prepare a suitable home for his beloved. This home would reflect upon his love and value that he placed on his bride. Typically, the groom would build an addition to his father's home. After his father gave the final approval, then, and only then, could his son fetch his bride and bring her to their new dwelling place. This initiates the third phase, the fetching of the bride.

With this in mind let's consider the words of Yeshua to His disciples just before He died as the Lamb of God to pay the bride price and return to His Father's house. In John 14, Messiah not only tells His disciples that He is going away, but He also tells them what He will be doing while He is away from them. Messiah assures them that even after He is gone from this earth that He will return and He will bring them to His Father's home. He tells them not to be worried or anxious. In light of this hope, He will be busy preparing an eternal home for them. We read in John 14:1-3,

> "Let not your heart be troubled; believe in God, believe also in Me. In My Father's house are many dwelling places; if it were not so, I would have told you; for I go to prepare a place for you. If I go and prepare a place for you, I will come again and receive you to Myself, that where I am, there you may be also."

Here we see the parallel of the groom preparing a place for his bride in his father's home. When the time is right, He will return and bring His bride there to be with Him. It is important to recognize that even Messiah, our Groom, did not know the exact time that He would return for His bride. When His disciples were growing impatient, in eager anticipation for the establishment of the Messianic Kingdom, they pressed Yeshua to give them an idea of when He would return. Yeshua answered,

> "But of that day and hour no one knows, not even the angels of heaven, nor the Son, but the Father alone." Matthew 24:36.

In Jewish tradition the groom's coming was to be so unexpected and unpredictable. It was customary for the groom to snatch his bride at night with excitement, noise, and blazing torches lighting the way. The parable of the ten virgins illustrates this tradition. It clearly communicates the sense of suddenness at the groom's appearance and the needed readiness of the Bride (Matthew 25:1-13).

This parable exemplifies the need for vigilance. For it says in Matthew 25:6, "But at midnight there was a shout, 'Behold, the bridegroom! Come out to meet him.'" The parable concludes that those who were prepared were being invited in and those who were not ready were being left out.

> Matthew 25:10-13, "The bridegroom came, and those who were ready went in with him to the wedding feast; and the door was shut. Later the other virgins also came, saying, 'Lord, lord, open up for us.' But he answered, 'Truly I say to you, I do not know you.' Be on the alert then, for you do not know the day nor the hour.'"

HEAVENLY SHOUT

In the New Covenant, the snatching away of the Bride has a specific name and it is commonly known by the term, the rapture. One of the main Scriptures that teach on the rapture of believers is found in 1 Thessalonians 4:16-17.

> "For the Lord Himself will come down from heaven with a shout, with the voice of the archangel and with the trumpet of God, and the dead in Messiah will rise first. Then we who are alive and remain will be caught up [raptured] together with them in the clouds to meet the Lord in the air, and so we shall always be with the Lord."

It's important to understand the context of this portion. In the beginning of Paul's letter he commends this congregation regarding their new life style. After becoming believers they turned from idols to serve the living and true God. Paul then connects this life of serving God with the betrothal waiting period. He exhorts them in 1 Thessalonians 1:9-10,

> "For they themselves report about us what kind of a reception we had with you, and how you turned to God from idols to serve a living and true God, and to wait for His Son from heaven, whom He raised from the dead, that is Yeshua, who delivers us from the wrath to come."

The phrase "to wait" in this passage stresses the idea of a certain eagerness. In this waiting, it implies a state of readiness on the part of the Thessalonians.

In verse 9 they were commended as serving the Lord faithfully. After these believers in the congregation at Thessalonica came to faith in the true and living God, they found a sense of expectancy concerning the future. While they were serving the true and living God, they also lived in the hope of the imminent return of Messiah Yeshua, which as we learned, is the fetching of the bride or the rapture. This is our glorious future.

> 1 Thessalonians 4:16, "For the Lord himself will descend from heaven with a shout, with the voice of the archangel and with the trumpet of God, and the dead in Messiah will rise first."

SUDDEN APPEARING

Note that this is a personal appearance of the Lord himself. Messiah will leave His position where He sits enthroned at the right hand of God the Father (Romans 8:34, Ephesians 1:20 and Colossians 3:1). The shout implies authority and urgency and is followed by the voice of the archangel and the great shofar of God.

The shofar of God is spoken of in 1 Corinthians 15:51-53, which is a parallel portion regarding the rapture of the Bride of Messiah.

> 1 Corinthians 15:51-53, "Behold, I tell you a mystery; we shall not all sleep, but we will all be changed, in a moment, in the twinkling of an eye, at the last shofar; for the trumpet will sound, and the dead will be raised imperishable, and we will be changed. For this perishable must put on the imperishable, and this mortal must put on immortality."

The sound of the trumpet will be a clear signal to the believers; both to those who have died and those who are still alive to meet the Lord in the air. What a wonderful event to live for, to anticipate, to contemplate, and to absolutely expect even in our lifetime.

This anticipation of the return of Yeshua characterized the body of Messiah, His bride from the very beginning. The teaching of living in readiness for Messiah's return permeated the teaching of the apostles.

Paul taught the believers at Philippi to understand that they were to live in light of the return of Messiah Yeshua. As we read in Philippians 3:20-21,

> "For our citizenship is in heaven, from which also we eagerly wait for a Savior, the Lord Yeshua the Messiah; who will transform the body of our humble state into conformity with the body of His glory, by the exertion of the power that He has even to subject all things to Himself."

CULTURE DIVINE

The beloved apostle John was trying to encourage the believers. In light of the false teachers he reminds them of the love of God and the coming of Messiah.

> 1 John 3:1-3, "See how great a love the Father has bestowed upon us, that we would be called children of God; and such we are. For this reason the world does not know us, because it did not know Him. Beloved, now we are children of God, and it has not appeared as yet what we will be. We know that when He appears, we will be like Him, because we shall see Him just as

> He is. And everyone who has this hope fixed on Him purifies himself, just as He is pure."

Another translation says, "Behold, what manner of love." This phrase expresses a question of amazement; what sort of love is this? The answer is saying that the love expressed is the very culture of heaven that reflects the God of love.

In verse two John goes on to say that now we are children of God. The word that is emphasized is "now", meaning that this eternal life belongs to us now. We don't have to wait until we die or we are fetched away as His bride to get it. We are born into the family of God and His everlasting life belongs to us currently.

This present eternal life means we are His bride and we are daughters of the King of kings. All of His glory and promises are for us to enjoy and utilize as we are valued and eternally desired by Him. Although these things are true, we do not look any different than others around us who do not have eternal life. Today, just as in the days of Yeshua, God's life is "veiled in flesh."

What will it be like when Messiah returns and we experience the plan that God has for us? What is it like for our family and friends who have gone to be with the Lord? These questions are shrouded in mystery.

> 1 John 3:2-3, "…And it has not appeared as yet what we will be. We know that, when He appears, we will be like Him, because we will see Him just as He is. And everyone who has this hope fixed on Him purifies himself, just as He is pure."

It does not yet appear or is not yet known what we shall be. All these things are producing an eternal weight of glory, not for this life only, but for eternal life so that we will be ready for the values of heaven.

Let us understand that these verses in 1 John are instructing us that this blessed hope and expectation of our Groom's return is purifying. We have several areas of certainty that should keep us eagerly waiting for His return.

As surely as He came the first time, He is returning the second time as all of history is moving toward this goal. All of the circumstances of this world are creating the conditions that Scripture predict. God is ultimately in control and working out His purposes.

WE WILL BE LIKE HIM

The groaning and weakness which we experience each day will be forgotten when our bodies are changed to be like His. The body is only a shell of the inner life. We do not suddenly change our entire character and personality when we see Yeshua. John is saying, what we have been becoming through the years of our life will suddenly be revealed when our Groom appears. Gradually, little by little, step by step, we will start to be like Him. The full extent to which we have become like Him will be revealed when we see Him, not before.

The question is, of course, how much of my life is becoming like Him right now? What percentage of time, as a believer, am I reflecting the values of Messiah and the culture of heaven?

1 John 3:3, "And everyone who has this hope fixed on Him purifies himself, just as He is pure."

If the degree to which you become like Him is the degree to which you will see Him as He is, then what a powerful motivation this is to become like Him now. Accept your circumstances and stop arguing with God. Begin to give thanks in all things, allowing these unique instruments of God's grace to do their work in your life.

God desires to use all the events of your life to conform you to the image of Messiah. He wants to use the great and the small, the mundane and the marvelous, and the oys and joys to grow you into the character of God's patience as Paul put it this way in Romans 5:3-5,

> "And not only this, but we also exult in our tribulations, knowing that tribulation brings about perseverance; and perseverance, proven character; and proven character, hope; and hope does not disappoint, because the love of God has been poured out within our hearts through the Holy Spirit who was given to us."

What does it mean that tribulation produces perseverance or patience? Our problems make us ready to wait, watch, and pray for God to work things out. This patience produces character as you experience God working things out. Again and again you see that the situations which caused you to fear, or made you uncertain, turned around as you patiently waited and looked to God to answer your prayers. As your prayers are answered, the experience of trusting in a faithful God produces hope.

In Hebrew, hope is translated *tikvah*, and means an absolute assurance or hope of certainty. Paul teaches from Romans 8:28,

> "And we know that God causes all things to work together for good to those who love God, to those who are called according to His purpose."

We don't always understand why things happen the way they do and why God allows certain outcomes. Here is where our faith and patience is tested and needs to be strengthened. Messiah, your Groom, is coming back for you. It is an absolute certainty. He is coming to fetch you. Are you waiting eagerly for His return? Are you making yourself ready for His appearing?

QUESTIONS AND REFLECTIONS:

1. Why is the third step in the Jewish wedding so unpredictable?

2. Reflect on the results of King Saul's impatience and disobedience to God and take time to consider your own life. Are you becoming impatient and feel like God is not answering your prayers?

3. In John 14:1-3 why did Yeshua speak to His disciples about being troubled and how did He reassure them?

4. How does the fact that Yeshua is coming for you keep you pure? (1 John 3:3)

Let us rejoice and be glad and give the glory to Him, for the marriage of the Lamb has come and His bride has made herself ready.
  Revelation 19:7

Chapter 4

Ultimate Celebration

Marriage Supper of the Lamb

A wedding will change the life of the bride forever even as vows are exchanged in front of the witnesses of family and friends. These vows state that they will live together "for better or worse, for richer or poorer, in sickness and in health..." The lives of both the bride and the groom will never be the same as they look toward their future together. In many Jewish weddings today there is a passage of Scripture from Jeremiah which encapsulates the sentiment of joy and gladness that a wedding can bring and are included as one of the Seven blessings (*Shevah Barchot*) recited during the wedding ceremony. Here God is depicting the restoration of Israel as he describes a time of utter waste and desolation that is transformed into a scene of total blessing and joy. God speaks of the joy of a wedding where the voices of the groom and the bride signify this restoration and vibrant life. Once again voice of joy shall be heard is based on Jeremiah 33:10-11.

> "Thus says the LORD, 'Yet again there will be heard in this place, of which you say, "It is a waste, without man and without beast," that is, in the cities of Judah and in the streets of Jerusalem that are desolate, without man and without inhabitant and without beast, the voice of joy and the voice of gladness, the voice of the bridegroom and the voice of the bride."

ONCE UPON A TIME IN THE GARDEN OF EDEN

Let's consider for a moment that we are time travelers and together we will go back to the beginning of creation, back to Genesis. When the Lord created the world in six days, all was good. Throughout the first chapter of Genesis the phrase "and God saw that it was good", is repeated again and again. After creating man in His image, in Genesis 2:18 God says, "It is not good for man to be alone." Consequently, God created a woman from Adam's rib and declared that they will be one flesh. Their oneness and unity was to reflect the joy of companionship found in the presence of the Triune God of Israel. This first marriage relationship was to be God's example of what unity and joy should look like.

Adam and Eve were in *Gan Eden* (the Garden of Eden). The Garden of Eden was God's sanctuary, the place of His presence which was a place of fruitfulness and perfection. Yet after sin entered in through their disobedience, Adam and Eve were cast out of *Gan Eden,* never to eat of the luscious fruit that had been so freely provided but rather to toil and taste the destructive power of sin. Instead of joy there was sorrow, instead of fruitfulness there was devastation.

JOY AND GLADNESS

In Jeremiah 33:10-11 God gives hope of restoration. He declares that once again (*od yishama*) there will be heard the sound of joy and gladness. The prophet Jeremiah speaks of a future time when Israel will be restored and healed.

These voices will not carry the cries of mourning, but the sound of laughter and great delight. In fact, the joy of a wedding is the symbol of the blessing of God; a thermometer to gauge the temperature of joy and gladness. Two different Hebrew words express the joy of the wedding in this passage: the voice of joy, *kol sasson,* and the voice of gladness, *kol simcha.*

The voice of joy, or *sasson,* means exultation and rejoicing. One of the many portions of Scripture to describe this kind of joy is found in Psalm 51:12 where King David prays: "Restore to me the joy *(sasson)* of Your salvation."

The word for gladness, or *simcha,* carries the idea of exceeding delight, extreme rejoicing and pleasure. In Jewish life, this word, *simcha,* is a popular word utilized in both Hebrew and Yiddish for a festive occasion, a time to rejoice.

Psalm 30:11, "King David wrote, "You have turned for me my mourning into dancing; You have loosed my sackcloth and girded me with gladness *(simcha)*."

As time travelers, let us be transported to the place of the *Greatest Simcha* of all. To the throne room of heaven we are transported first. To the celebrations of the ages that are yet to come. We come to a wedding celebration described in Revelation, the final book of the Bible.

Significantly, this celebration will be the culmination of God's plan for us. What began in Genesis in that first marriage that was marred by sin will now be restored because "the marriage of the Lamb has come and His bride has made herself ready" (Revelation 19:7).

OVERVIEW OF JEWISH WEDDING CUSTOMS

Remember how we arrived at this marriage feast. During the first phase called the Arrangement or, *Shiddukhin*, we were chosen by our heavenly matchmaker reminding us of our immeasurable value to our Groom. After the *Shiddukhin* we entered the *Eyrusin* or betrothal period and realized that the time of preparation meant that everything we do matters while we wait.

The third mysterious and unpredictable phase is called the Fetching of the Bride. In this period of time we are preparing for our Groom to return, just as He is preparing an eternal home for us as His Bride.

As we come to the actual marriage of the Lamb we will glimpse into our future together. We are transported with John into the heavenlies as we consider this wedding celebration in its Scriptural context. Our wedding ceremony is preceded by the ultimate worship scene found in Revelation 19:1 where we read, "After these things."

FOUR-FOLD HALLELUJAH

When John says, "after these things," he is referring to the fact that Messiah Yeshua has conquered the enemies of God, the harlot, the demonic world system, and all who would stand against the Kingdom of our Groom. These enemies who were the counterfeit gods and deceived many, which came only to destroy and enslave, have been defeated. Now, just before our wedding ceremony begins we have the declaration that our Groom has made right everything that was wrong.

The realization that Yeshua the righteous King is victorious brings an incredible heavenly response. John begins in Revelation 19:1,

> "After these things I heard something like a loud voice of a great multitude in heaven saying "Hallelujah! Salvation and glory and power belong to our God."

This is the first Hallelujah of four that we will find in Revelation 19. Hallelujah is a compound word from *Hallel* (praise) and *Yah*, the covenant name of God, *Yahweh*. It was intriguing for me to discover, that although hallelujah is found numerous times in the Hebrew Scriptures, especially throughout the Psalms, this passage in Revelation is the only time that Hallelujah appears in the New Covenant. How appropriate that the praise for God is to be proclaimed from heaven for this auspicious moment.

These Hallelujahs reveal an amazing heavenly scene recorded by the beloved apostle John that is leading up to the party of all parties, our wedding celebration. Revelation 19:2 gives the reason for this heavenly outburst of praise,

> "Because His judgments are true and righteous; for He has judged the great harlot who was corrupting the earth with her immorality, and He has avenged the blood of His bond-servants on her."

Our King Messiah is the only one who can accomplish this justice because He is the only true and righteous judge. He is the LORD our Righteousness, *Jehovah-Tzikenu*. He has brought His righteous judgment on those who have come against Him and His servants.

After this first Hallelujah we have the second and third Hallelujahs encompassing the fact that God's judgment is complete. In response to this declaration it says that the twenty four elders and the four living creatures around the throne fall down to worship the Holy God of Israel.

> Revelation 19:3-4, "And a second time they said, "Hallelujah! Her smoke rises up forever and ever." And the twenty-four elders and the four living creatures fell down and worshiped God who sits on the throne saying, "Amen. Hallelujah!"

What an astounding scene as heaven is rocking with praise because God's eternal and righteous judgment is acknowledged. Now the first three Hallelujahs have escalated from relief. There is great rejoicing and liberation to hear that the evil world system has been overthrown.

However, the fourth Hallelujah is different. This final Hallelujah is a limitless expression of joy and delight as the reign of the Lord our God, the Almighty, is recognized. All authority, all strength, and all power are attributed to Him. In Revelation 19:5 a voice from the throne of God invites everyone to join in jubilant praise,

> "And a voice came from the throne, saying, Give praise to our God, all you His bond-servants, you who fear Him, the small and the great."

This verse should inspire each of us as His servants in His Kingdom because we are in awe of Him from the least of us to the greatest of us. None of us are insignificant in His Kingdom. Today you may feel insignificant or overlooked in your earthly labors, but the truth is you are of great value to God and at the wedding ceremony your significance will be revealed and realized. Whether you are older or younger in years or a mature believer or just new in the faith, it does not matter because you are important to God. He chose you as His treasured possession and He has plans for you not just here on earth but for eternity. This is why the life we have in Him is called eternal life.

This future hope does not depend on your mood or frame of mind or even the season of your life, but rather this hope is determined by the sure Word of the Lord. Our hope and confident expectation is built on the promises of the Word of God.

Can you imagine this mighty response to the call of God as all the voices unite together? What do all these voices sound like as they are raised together? What will your voice sound like? In Revelation 9:6 John goes on to explain, "Then I heard something like the voice of a great multitude and like the sound of many waters and like the sound of mighty peals of thunder, saying, "Hallelujah! For the Lord our God, the Almighty, reigns."

The sound of many waters, could this be comparable to Niagara Falls to the billionth degree? The tremendous noise of the waters was accompanied by mighty peals of thunder, like a thunderous voice in one accord. This deafening blast would shake the entire universe affirming that indeed our God reigns. He is establishing His Kingdom, the eternal Kingdom where we will be forever with our King, our Groom, and our Messiah. For now, we are approaching that climatic event, awaited by God the Father and the Bridegroom His Son. Are you ready for this tremendous celebration? It might surprise you as it did me to realize who exactly will be there at this party. We, His bride, along with a great cloud of witnesses, will be there.

WITNESSES AT THE WEDDING

Consider with me for a moment the one who prepared the way of our Groom and called himself a friend of the Groom. John the Baptizer was questioned about this Yeshua who was immersing John's disciples. His disciples were confused regarding Yeshua's authority to immerse others because it seemed to be in competition for what John was already doing. John the Baptizer quickly told these disciples, "Listen, I'm not the Messiah, my calling was to announce that the Messiah is here" I proclaimed, "Behold the Lamb of God who takes away the sin of the world" (John 1:29).

John the Baptizer goes on to give an example to his followers. In John 3:28-30 he says,

> "You yourselves are my witnesses that I said, 'I am not the Messiah,' but, 'I have been sent ahead of Him.' He who has the bride is the bridegroom; but the friend of the bridegroom, who stands and hears him, rejoices greatly because of the bridegroom's voice. So this joy of mine has been made full."

John explains that he is not the bridegroom but the friend of the groom, much like the best man. The best man does not complain that he is not the groom but is there to assist the bridegroom in every way possible. As a friend of the groom he is satisfied to see the wedding successfully completed, to be a witness at the wedding.

John was killed by Herod early in his ministry. As the final prophet to Israel, he was not part of what happened on Pentecost/*Shavuot* when the fullness of the Holy Spirit came upon the believers. In Acts 2, at *Shavuot*, the believers became one body; Jews and Gentiles were one in Messiah as His bride.

Now consider with me Hebrews 11 and 12 where we find the heroes of the faith that were also called witnesses. The list includes Abraham, Noah, Sarah, Moses, David, and many others. Like John the Baptizer these heroes of the faith were not part of the Bride of Messiah, but were friends or witnesses of the wedding between the Messiah and His Bride. We have wonderful heroes who will be witnesses at the marriage of the Lamb.

The writer of the book of Hebrews wanted us, as His bride, to understand that we have these witnesses surrounding us. In light of having these heroes of the faith who are friends of the bride, we have an exhortation to follow.

> Hebrews 12:1-3, "Therefore, since we have so great a cloud of witnesses surrounding us, let us also lay aside every encumbrance and the sin which so easily entangles us, and let us run with endurance the race that is set before us, fixing our eyes on Yeshua, the author and perfecter of faith, who for the joy set before Him endured the cross, despising the shame, and has sat down at the right hand of the throne of God. For consider Him who has endured such hostility by sinners against Himself, so that you will not grow weary and lose heart."

This race is our lives now as we are in the betrothal period waiting for our groom to return. Sometimes this life can feel like a crawl, a standstill even, but God is always at work and what we do each day matters.

Therefore, we should not try to navigate this betrothal time with any encumbrances. Imagine yourself trying to run a race with 50 pound ankle weights. Perhaps you are trying to run this race for Yeshua with the burden of guilt and sorrow that is heavier than a 50 pound ankle weight. Lay this burden down and cast your cares on Yeshua.

Hebrews 12:1 also tells us to get rid of the sin that so easily ensnares you. Do not let sin deter you from an intimate walk with Yeshua. Confess your anger, your bitterness, and your jealousy to God. He will cleanse us so that we can run the race with our eyes on Yeshua. If we keep our eyes on Him (Hebrews 12:2), we have the promise of our Groom that we will not grow weary or lose our enthusiasm.

While here on earth, Yeshua had to remind His followers not to lose heart and not to be troubled. In fact, the most frequent exhortation that Yeshua gave during His earthly ministry had to do with telling His followers not to be afraid. Fear not and don't be anxious about anything. Over and over again He tells us that if we put Him and His kingdom first, everything else will be added to us. Why do you think that Messiah had to remind His disciples so often to "not be afraid, and don't let your hearts be troubled?" We are just as insecure and afraid as the first century believers.

For us today we need to constantly be reminded that God truly does have everything under His control. I need to stop being anxious and instead choose to acknowledge each day that He is Lord, He is my Groom, and I will trust Him. It is a choice to live by faith and not by fear. We can live in confidence and eager anticipation because we know the future is in His capable hands. Remember the great cloud of witnesses that are around you.

In the heavenly scene found in Revelation 19 we see who will be there at the marriage of the Lamb. It is the Bride that is made up of all of us who follow the Messiah and the witnesses or friends of the bride. We have a heavenly glimpse of the joy that awaits us.

SAY YES TO THE DRESS

Have you noticed the plethora of TV shows that highlight the importance of having just the right wedding dress no matter the cost? When interviewed, one woman said she had been dreaming of her wedding dress since she was a little girl and wanted to look like a queen when she walked down the aisle. In Revelation 19:7-8 it tells us that what we wear matters. We discover that right there in heaven the wedding dress is not only mentioned, but is also vitally important for what this dress represents.

> Revelation 19:7-8, "...the marriage of the Lamb has come and His bride has made herself ready." It was given to her to clothe herself in fine linen, bright and clean; for the fine linen is the righteous acts of the saints."

Verse 8 gives us a picture of the clothing of the bride made of fine linen. This fine linen represents the most beautiful and exquisite of fabrics. It is the clothing made up of the righteous deeds of the bride while on earth. This external clothing is a result of being filled with the Holy Spirit. The deeds that we are doing on earth should, in essence, reflect the very character of God in your life; His fruit of love, joy, peace, patience, kindness, and goodness. Each day we can anticipate the celebration with our groom and live in light of how blessed we are.

> Revelation 19:9, Then He said to me, "Write, 'Blessed are those who are invited to the marriage supper of the Lamb.'" And he said to me, "These are true words of God."

In Revelation 9:11 John describes our Groom, "And I saw heaven opened, and behold, a white horse, and He who sat on it is called Faithful and True, and in righteousness He judges and wages war." Yeshua the Messiah is our conquering hero who comes to make all things right.

We began this chapter by noting that at the first wedding, Adam and Eve were cast out of *Gan Eden,* and God initiated His plan to redeem and restore us back to Himself. Here in Revelation 21 we are invited to enter into our new home that our Groom has prepared for us. We will eat freely of the fruit of the tree of life because of what our Groom has done for us. There shall no longer be any curse and the throne of God and the Lamb shall be in our new dwelling place. Imagine you are there with John and you are seeing your new home for the first time.

> Revelation 21:1-5, "Then I saw a new heaven and a new earth; for the first heaven and the first earth passed away, and there is no longer any sea. And I saw the holy city, New Jerusalem, coming down out of heaven from God, made ready as a bride adorned for her husband. And I heard a loud voice from the throne, saying, "Behold, the tabernacle of God is among men, and He shall dwell among them, and they shall be His people, and God Himself will be among them, and He will wipe away every tear from their eyes; and there will no longer be any death; there will no longer be any mourning, or crying, or pain; the first things have passed away." And He who sits on the throne said, "Behold, I am making all things new." And He said, "Write, for these words are faithful and true."

Ultimate Celebration

QUESTIONS AND REFLECTIONS:

1. What gives you the most joy in your life right now?

2. According to Revelation 19 can you picture yourself in heaven shouting Hallelujah?

3. Who are the witnesses at the Marriage of the Lamb?

4. Consider your wedding dress and how you are preparing for your ultimate celebration.

*Your throne, O God, is forever and ever;
A scepter of uprightness is the scepter of Your
kingdom. You have loved righteousness and
hated wickedness; Therefore God, Your God,
has anointed You with the oil of joy above Your
fellows. All Your garments are fragrant with
myrrh and aloes and cassia; Out of ivory palaces
stringed instruments have made You glad.
Psalm 45:6-8*

Chapter 5

The Song Of Love

Your Perfect Groom

*I*n our society today, weddings are one of the most celebratory ceremonies. If you could envision a perfect wedding, what would come to your mind as to how the event would unfold? At a typical wedding the groom comes in almost unnoticed; taking his place in the front, by the *chuppah* or canopy, expectantly waiting for his bride. The bridal procession begins with a very cute flower girl shuffling through the rose petals that have been strategically placed for the bride's arrival. Then there are the bridesmaids who march down the aisle with elegant gowns and floral bouquets. Musicians serenade the guests while anticipation intensifies. Suddenly, the music changes and everyone stands up, peering expectantly back down the aisle hoping for a glimpse of the bride in her dress. Finally, the bride appears slowly walking down the aisle on her father's arm. The bride's entrance is the climactic moment of the whole processional, and signals to all that the ceremony is now ready to begin because the bride has arrived. She could not be any happier. After all, she has found the groom of her dreams.

This captivation with weddings comes as no surprise to our Creator, who is the Author of marriage. God Himself planted in us the desire to find a perfect match, to love, and to be loved.

Perhaps this is how we are acculturated to weddings here on earth, but in heaven we might be a bit surprised as to how the wedding ceremony is performed. In Psalm 45, we find an incredible look at a royal wedding. Like a best-kept secret, this Psalm may often be overlooked by the reader, yet it is a profoundly eye-opening passage. It contains a description of the royal wedding. If we could stretch our imagination and list the supreme qualities for the perfect Groom to be, what it would look like?

In this chapter we will take a look at the most desirable groom of all. Today, as single individuals long to find the perfect companion, we have various matchmaking sites springing up. I suggest that we already have a site where we can find our perfect match, and it is found in the ancient resources of the Scriptures. We will uncover the ageless secrets that bring ultimate fulfillment. Can you imagine finding a spouse with all the following qualities: Someone who is good looking, gracious in his speech, a heroic warrior, and coming on a white horse to rescue you? One that always tells the truth, humble and blameless, a great teacher of awesome instruction, a protector and conqueror of evil, a rich king with a throne that is eternal, well dressed, and smells really good? Can this even be possible in the best of fairytales? I believe that our Heavenly Matchmaker has provided this and so much more. We should never settle for less than our heavenly Father has in store for each of us. In this chapter we will learn about our perfect groom who fits all of our ideal expectations. As we take a closer look at Psalm 45 I hope that you will agree that it is truly the picture of the perfect groom. For in this passage of Scripture we will see the qualities detailed out in the life of One who will never disappoint us and fits the description above.

A SONG OF LOVE

Psalm 45:1-11, "For the choir director; according to the *Shoshannim*. A Maskil of the sons of Korah. A Song of Love.

1. My heart overflows with a good theme; I address my verses to the King; My tongue is the pen of a ready writer.

You are fairer than the sons of men; Grace is poured upon Your lips; Therefore God has blessed You forever.

3. Gird Your sword on Your thigh, O Mighty One, In Your splendor and Your majesty!

4. And in Your majesty ride on victoriously, For the cause of truth and meekness and righteousness; Let Your right hand teach You awesome things.

5. Your arrows are sharp; The peoples fall under You;

Your arrows are in the heart of the King's enemies.

6. Your throne, O God, is forever and ever; A scepter of uprightness is the scepter of Your kingdom.

7. You have loved righteousness and hated wickedness; Therefore God, Your God, has anointed You With the oil of joy above Your fellows.

8. All Your garments are fragrant with myrrh and aloes and cassia; Out of ivory palaces stringed instruments have made You glad.

9. Kings' daughters are among Your noble ladies; At Your right hand stands the queen in gold from Ophir.

10. Listen, O daughter, give attention and incline your ear: Forget your people and your father's house;

11. Then the King will desire your beauty. Because He is your Lord, bow down to Him."

A LITTLE BACKGROUND

The Psalm begins for the choir director or chief musician, which means that this Psalm was written by a Temple worship leader such as Asaph, Heman, or Ethan. The phrase "according to" or "upon the Shoshannim," literally means "upon the lilies" and indicates that it is a love song for the springtime when all things are becoming new again. The winter is past and the new birth is here.

In this introduction, the sons of Korah or *L'benai-Korah,* implies that this song is for the Levitical choir in the Temple. This song is also called a Maschil, which is a Hebrew word that means wisdom or instruction that is put to music.

As we study this Psalm we will discover God's wisdom for our lives. Lastly, this Psalm is called "A Song of Loves" or *yedidot*. As a love song, Psalm 45 evidently celebrates the marriage of an acclaimed king. Various names such as "Solomon" are suggested by commentators for the king, but even Solomon is unworthy of this apparent Messianic description of a King. This is an elevated spiritual love song where we will discover that the writer is using earthly language to describe celestial or heavenly things. He is describing a wedding event with its local colorings that are looking forward and anticipating the marriage of the King of kings.

This Psalm is intended to show us how to love Him who first loved us. This song unfolds with a portrayal of His coming forth after His marriage with us, His bride, to deal with His enemies and to reign over the nations. In verses 1-8 we have the description of His Royal Majesty, our Groom. This worship leader is totally inspired as he begins,

> "My heart overflows with a good theme; I address my verses to the King; My tongue is the pen of a ready writer" (Psalm 45:1).

The writer states that his heart is overflowing with a good theme. The word for "good" in Hebrew is *tov*, a common word used throughout the Scriptures. In the case of Psalm 45, this good subject matter is about the King of kings and it is understood to speak of the character of God.

Many times in the Scriptures we are instructed to "Give thanks to the Lord for He is good, (*tov*), His mercies forever endure" (Psalm 118:1).

Goodness is a character quality of God that comes from God. If the worship writer is inspired about a good theme or topic, it has to reflect who God is and His words of love for us.

Notice how the thoughts come pouring out and from the abundance of his heart his mouth speaks. Have you ever felt so excited about something you just had to share it? Here we have the idea of the words bubbling up from this inspired writer who can't get the words out fast enough. This is what I want for my heart. I desire to overflow with excitement for what Yeshua has done for me. I yearn to have this enthusiasm for Yeshua well up, first from my heart, then in my speech, that it may give grace and overflow into the lives of others.

But what is overflowing from this worship leader's heart? From verse two we understand that this King is really good looking when the poet sings, "You art fairer than the sons of men." The Complete Jewish Bible translates this verse,

> "You are the most handsome of men; gracious speech flows from your lips. For God has blessed you forever."

In Psalm 45:3 the word for fairer, handsome, or beautiful is *yaffe*. Here we have a comparison that he is not only beautiful, this King is beautiful beyond description. This phrase brings to mind a worship song, *I Stand In Awe of You* (by Hillsong United) that never fails to inspire me.

> You are beautiful beyond description
> Too marvelous for words
> Too wonderful of comprehension

> Like nothing ever seen or heard
> Who can grasp your infinite wisdom
> Who can fathom the depth of your love
> You are beautiful beyond description
> Majesty enthroned above
>
> And I stand, I stand in awe of you
> I stand, I stand in awe of you
> Holy God to whom all praise is due
> I stand in awe of you.

How different from His first coming where the prophet Isaiah says about our King, "And when we shall see Him, there is no beauty in Him that we should desire Him." (Isaiah 53:2). When Yeshua came to earth He laid aside the glory He had with the Father before the world began. When He stepped out of eternity into time He was robed in human flesh, and was born of a woman in a lowly stable. In fact, the second verse of I Stand in Awe of You describes His first coming in this way:

> You are beautiful beyond description
> Yet God crushed You for my sin
> In agony and deep affliction
> Cut off that I might enter in
>
> Who can grasp such tender compassion?
> Who can fathom this mercy so free?
> You are beautiful beyond description
> Lamb of God who died for me

How beautiful He is! He is *yaffe meod* - very beautiful.

GRACIOUS SPEECH

Psalm 45 verse 2 goes on to describe our groom's speech.

"Grace (*chesed*) is poured upon Your lips; Therefore God has blessed You forever."

Here we discover that our Groom is always gracious in His speaking because He is blessed eternally. When Messiah began His earthly ministry, the report of those who heard Him was one of amazement:

"And all were speaking well of Him, and wondering at the gracious words which were falling from His lips; and they were saying, "Is this not Joseph's son?"(Luke 4:22).

His grace expressed itself in every aspect of His character, His conduct, and His conversation. The grace which was poured into His life was poured out of His lips. Are you in need of His gracious words to you, His favor, His understanding of your life? Be assured that He not only sees you but He also cares about what you are going through. The writer to the Hebrews tells us that our High Priest is always there to help us in our time of need,

Hebrews 4:15-16, "For we do not have a high priest who cannot sympathize with our weaknesses, but One who has been tempted in all things as we are, yet without sin. Let us therefore draw near with confidence to the throne of grace, that we may receive mercy and may find grace to help in time of need."

Being gracious is such a wonderful expression of God's love. Can you imagine always having the right words to say that would minister grace to the hearer? This is exactly what our Groom desires for each of us in our lives. When we depend on His grace, our lives are overflowing into the lives of others. Just as we are exhorted to do by Paul,

> Ephesians 4:29, "Let no unwholesome word proceed from your mouth, but only such a word as is good for edification according to the need of the moment, that it may give grace to those who hear."

I NEED A HERO

I remember when I was a child making a flower wreath for my hair and pretending that I was a princess. As a princess, I was waiting for my prince to come for me and sweep me off my feet. How many of you have dreamed to have a prince come riding on his white horse to first rescue you from all your problems then take you to his castle where you would live happily ever after?

In 1984 a song entitled *Holding Out for a Hero* was recorded by Bonnie Tyler. This popular secular song gave voice to many of us who were looking for a hero. The verse and the chorus echoed the sentiment that a hero is hard to find.

> Where have all the good men gone
> And where are all the gods?
> Where's the street-wise Hercules
> To fight the rising odds?
> Isn't there a white knight upon a fiery steed?
> Late at night I toss and turn and dream
> of what I need

> **[Chorus]** I need a hero
> I'm holding out for a hero 'til the end of the night
> He's gotta be strong
> And he's gotta be fast
> And he's gotta be fresh from the fight
> I need a hero
> I'm holding out for a hero 'til the morning light
> He's gotta be sure
> And it's gotta be soon
> And he's gotta be larger than life

Most of us are aware that the stark reality is that we will never find such a hero on this earth. However, there is great news for followers of Yeshua the Messiah because He is our heavenly hero. He is the One found in Psalm 45 who is the source for what are hearts are continually longing for. In verses 3 through 5 we are given some specifics as to how Yeshua, our hero, can meet our needs. He is the One who comes riding victoriously on his horse to vanquish our enemies. He is the righteous One who will make all that is wrong in the world, right and true.

> Psalms 45:3-5, "Gird Your sword on Your thigh, O Mighty One, In Your splendor and Your majesty! And in Your majesty ride on victoriously, For the cause of truth and meekness and righteousness; Let Your right hand teach You awesome things. Your arrows are sharp; The peoples fall under You; Your arrows are in the heart of the King's enemies."

The title, "Mighty One," means hero or *gibbor* in Hebrew. Mighty God or *El Gibbor* is one of the prophetic names of Messiah found in Isaiah 9:6. He is described,

"For a child will be born to us, a son will be given to us; And the government will rest on His shoulders; And His name will be called Wonderful Counselor, Mighty God, Eternal Father, Prince of Peace."

RETURNING ON THE WHITE HORSE

In Revelation 19:11 we have a closer look at our Hero as John describes His coming to make all things right.

"And I saw heaven opened, and behold, a white horse, and He who sat upon it is called Faithful and True, and in righteousness He judges and wages war."

In Jewish society horses were considered mighty animals that conquering heroes would ride. In fact, in Jewish tradition the Messiah was expected to come as a conquering hero to deliver Israel from her enemies. This is one reason that many in Israel did not recognize Yeshua as Messiah.

At His first coming He entered Jerusalem, not as a victorious warrior on a magnificent steed, but rather as the humble King on a lowly donkey thus fulfilling the prophecy of Zechariah 9:9.

"Rejoice greatly, O daughter of Zion! Shout in triumph, O daughter of Jerusalem! Behold, your king is coming to you; He is just and endowed with salvation, Humble, and mounted on a donkey, Even on a colt, the foal of a donkey."

By contrast, in Psalm 45 verse 4 we have our Hero riding on victoriously, "For the cause of truth and meekness and righteousness."

Can you picture it? The Messiah of Israel is now the conquering Hero returning on His mighty white horse, not as the humble King, but as the triumphant One. All those who were against Him will be judged with truth and righteousness; For He is the Lord our righteousness.

These verses continue to proclaim that our hero is also our protector. If you are identified with your Groom then He will defend, protect, and secure you from all your enemies. You must rely on Him and not try to defend yourself, realizing that retribution belongs to the Lord. He will settle all accounts one day, making everything right that has been wrong.

AWE INSPIRING TEACHER

In Psalm 45:4, Yeshua is recognized as an awe-inspiring teacher when the worship leader declares, "let your right hand teach you awesome things." I need to ask myself each day, am I learning from my Groom today? Think of Mary and Martha who were not only disciples of Yeshua, but also such close friends that He felt comfortable in their home. The three times we meet Mary we find her sitting at the feet of Yeshua, learning from Him. In Luke 10:42, Messiah lovingly reminds Martha that Mary has chosen the good part that can never be taken away from her.

Learning at the feet of our King brings both daily sustenance and spiritual stability which yields eternal rewards. When the works which were done in His power and grace will stand the test of purification through the fires, and come out as silver and gold, we will receive those eternal rewards.

OUR RIGHTEOUS JUDGE

In Psalm 45:5, the idea of our King's absolute judgment upon His enemies is spoken of when His arrows pierce the hearts of those who stood against Him. His words pierce like a sword but enter into the heart like a well-aimed arrow. Likewise, John describes Messiah's future judgment upon the nations in Revelation 19:15-16. "From His mouth comes a sharp sword, so that with it He may strike down the nations, and He will rule them with a rod of iron; and He treads the wine press of the fierce wrath of God, the Almighty. And on His robe and on His thigh He has a name written, "KING OF KINGS, AND LORD OF LORDS."

THE FINAL WORD FROM HEAVEN

In Psalm 45:6-7, we have the proof that this Psalm is Messianic. These verses are repeated in Hebrews 1:8-9 where Yeshua is introduced as the final Word from God. An explanation is given as to how Yeshua our Messiah, our Groom, is the Eternal King who is higher than the created angels, and will be worshipped forever.

> Psalm 45:6-7, "Your throne, O God, is forever and ever; A scepter of uprightness is the scepter of Your kingdom. You have loved righteousness and hated wickedness; Therefore God, Your God, has anointed You with the oil of joy above Your fellows."

What a breathtaking consideration. We serve an Eternal King who has prepared for us an Eternal Kingdom. In Revelation 21 and 22 there is a description of our Eternal home which is the reality of our future.

We read of the glories that await us in His Kingdom and are given a glimpse of our eternal Kingdom with our eternal King. Sometimes I long for heaven and grow impatient. Yet I remember that I am still in the betrothal period with my Groom, therefore I not only need to be preparing for His return, but also have patience as I long to see Him face to face.

THE QUINTESSENTIAL AROMATHERAPY

In Psalm 45 verse 8 we see our King's clothing which smells wonderful and aromatic. These fragrances, myrrh for beauty, and aloes and cassia for healing, were mentioned throughout Yeshua's life. At His birth, the wise men came from the east and presented fragrant spices. His feet were anointed by Mary for His death and afterwards His body was wrapped with aromatic spices.

Now we find that all the King's garments are fragrant with myrrh and aloes and cassia. This has to be the quintessential aromatherapy. The second part of verse 8 states, "Out of ivory palaces stringed instruments have made You glad." These ivory palaces are the most lavish and opulent of all. Solomon had an ivory throne, but here we are told of ivory palaces. This joyous celebration is also filled with beautiful music.

THE PERFECT GROOM

This description of our Perfect Groom strikes a chord in my heart as I rejoice in realizing how this perfect match can minister and supply all my needs "according to His riches in glory in Messiah Yeshua." (Philippians 4:19). All of my physical desires are met in Him as I see Him, hear Him, touch Him, and even smell His fragrance. All of our emotional and spiritual aspects are answered in Him as He is victorious over evil. We have joy in our King in the celebration of our marriage, security in Him reigning in our lives, and ruling with Him from His ivory palaces.

After 8 verses of the description of the beauty and character and power of the King, our Perfect Groom, we come to the queen who is introduced in an almost casual off-handed manner, as a footnote to the King. Our thoughts are all taken up with the King! He has our undivided attention. We are thinking of Him and nothing else matters. Then we meet the queen:

> Psalm 45:9, "Kings' daughters are among Your noble ladies; At Your right hand stands the queen in gold from Ophir."

Our attention is turned to the queen and those who accompany her. We are standing with our King and this idea of standing at His right hand means that we are in a place of honor that is equal to our Groom. We are there to bring honor to the King and bring our attention to Him.

HIS DESIRE FOR YOU

Here in Psalm 45, the entrance of the bride is noted in connection with how the King will desire her. Because He is our eternal King, we have an eternal destiny. He makes our lives meaningful and rich. We have not chosen Him, but rather our heavenly Matchmaker chose us before the foundation of the world. We have responded to our Groom as we realize His eternal love for us. Our lives should be all about Him.

> Psalm 45:10, What does our Groom desire of us? "Listen, O daughter, give attention and incline your ear: Forget your people and your father's house."

The word "listen" in Hebrew is, *Sh'ma*, and means to hear with intent to obey. Think about how you teach your daughter to clean up her room. You give careful instructions as to what you expect and that you want the room cleaned by the end of the day. Your daughter looks like she is listening as she nods her head in agreement, yet at day's end her room is still a mess. What happened? Your daughter did not listen with the intent to obey or heed your directions. She was faking it and looking like she would obey, but really had no intention to follow through. Do we treat the Lord like this? What is it that we are obeying, understanding, and listening intently to? When the Lord tells us to listen or hear He expects us to heed, live out, and follow through with His teaching.

What does it mean "to forget your people and your father's house?" Psalm 45:10. Simply put, it means that the King must be primary in my life. Each of us must put Messiah first in all our relationships. We are to forget those old alliances and relationships that would hinder us from concentrating on the beauty and glory of our Groom. When we seek Him first and His Kingdom, then everything else will be added to us. Just as God has already blotted out our guilty past, so the King wants us to break with our past, our old affections, pains, and hurts. We are to cast all these burdens on Messiah and trust Him completely. We must be willing to look forward to our future. For now our affections must be toward our King, our Groom. As His bride, He must have priority in all your relationships. When this happens, we have a promise in verse 11, "Then the King will desire your beauty. Because He is your Lord, bow down to Him."

The same word for beauty began the Psalm when the Groom is described as fairer (*yaffe*) than the sons of men. Here as His bride, we reflect His beauty (*yaffa*). The Lord has made us beautiful and He loves us unconditionally.

Unless our beauty reflects this praise and reverence for God, it is empty and worthless. Proverbs 31:30 teaches us the same truth, "Charm is deceitful and beauty is vain, But a woman who fears the LORD, she shall be praised." However, when I am revealing my King's beauty in my devotion to Him, then I will be pleasing to Him.

Verse 11 continues "Because He is your Lord, bow down to Him." This position of prostration of falling on our faces signifies the total yielding and submission of our hearts to His authority, His Kingship, and His reign in our lives.

We can have a sure confidence that we will be with our Groom who is the Lover of our souls forever. We will be reigning with Him and rejoicing with Him for eternity. He is the One who is beautiful beyond description, too marvelous for words, and we stand in awe of Him. Make Him the focus of your life and you will find that He will supply all your needs according to the matchless riches of heaven.

As we lift our Groom up and give Him preeminence, He continually adds value to our lives. We are Eternally Desired by our Eternal King. Even as Messiah prays for us in John 17:24, we see His eternal desire, "Father, I desire that they also, whom You have given Me, be with Me where I am..."

We began this study reflecting on a modern day wedding where the bride is the center of attention. How different the marriage of the Lamb will be as our Groom, Hero, Protector, and Righteous One will command our attention and allegiance for all eternity.

QUESTIONS AND REFLECTIONS:

1. Personalize Psalm 45:10-11.

2. Consider anything that would take away from your devotion to your King and ask God to forgive you. Ask God to give you an undivided heart for Him.

3. Read Psalm 45 over several times and write out your own insights to describe your Perfect Groom.

4. Are you looking for a hero and if so what kind of hero would he be?

*Come, let us worship and bow down,
Let us kneel before the LORD our Maker.
For He is our God, and we are the people of
His pasture and the sheep of His hand.
Psalm 95:6-7*

Chapter 6

The Essence of Worship

The Heart of the Matter

In the previous chapter we took a close look at our Groom from Psalm 45. In Psalm 45:10-11 we are given the key to the most intimate relationship with our Groom, how we can live out our relationship day by day. This is essential as we are preparing for heaven while living here on earth.

> "Listen, O daughter, give attention and incline your ear; Forget your people and your father's house; then the King will desire your beauty; Because He is your Lord, bow down to Him."

In Psalm 45:10-11 we find the "leaving and cleaving" concept, complete abandonment of the past ties and absolute loyalty to the King. We can learn how to attach ourselves to the King while He is away and live out the qualities and values of the Kingdom to come. I believe that as we learn the art of worship, "bowing down to Him," we are preparing for the culture of heaven. Worshipping Messiah is the key for our lives and it is the heart of what we are to be doing while we wait for His return. In other words, because Messiah Yeshua is my King, my Lord, and my Groom, I will bow down and worship Him.

There is a popular song entitled, *The Heart of Worship*, with the phrase, "I'm coming back to the heart of worship and it's all about You, it's all about You, Jesus."

This song rings true does it not? The heart of the matter is worshiping Yeshua the King of Kings. In Psalm 45, we realize it is all about our Conquering Hero, our righteous and true King. If we can grasp the priority of worshipping the Lord in our walk with Him we will:

1. *Experience the intimacy of His presence* — "Abide in Me, and I in you" (John 15:4).

2. *Rest in His sustaining power* — "I can do all things through Messiah who gives me strength" (Philippians 4:13).

3. *Attain His perspective for our lives* — "For we are His workmanship, created in Christ Jesus for good works, which God prepared beforehand, that we should walk in them" (Ephesians 2:10).

We were chosen and appointed for His divine purposes. God, in fact, does all things with great intention. Consider the purpose of God's deliverance of the Hebrew slaves from bondage in Egypt. Assuring Moses, the Lord gave him the reason,

> "Certainly I will be with you, and this shall be the sign to you that it is I who have sent you: when you have brought the people out of Egypt, you shall worship God at this mountain" (Exodus 3:12).

Following God's call for His life, Moses pursued Pharaoh to grant permission for the Israelites to go and worship. Moses repeats the phrase "you shall worship God at this mountain" several times as he commands Pharaoh, "let my people go." Moses explained to Pharaoh that the purpose of their freedom was to be able to worship the One True God. In a similar way, why did God save us and deliver us from the bondage of sin?

Was it just for the pursuit of happiness and success so we can do our own thing? Although God makes us prosperous in what we do and gives us all things to enjoy, there is more to His redemptive purposes. He delivered us from the domain of darkness to the kingdom of His beloved Son so we could know Him, experience His love, and worship Him, the King of kings.

A TALE OF TWO SISTERS

This may sound simple and may even seem to be easy to do once you know the truth, but in reality it does not happen naturally, or habitually. We women are prone to worry and focus on our immediate needs and are tempted to troubleshoot and work especially on behalf of everyone else. Are we any different than women in the days of Yeshua? Let's take a visit to the home of Miriam and Martha in the village of Bethany, perhaps the favorite place of Yeshua to rest and enjoy a delicious meal during His earthly ministry. Let's take a look at the narrative found in Luke 10:38-42.

> "As they continued their travel, Yeshua entered a village. A woman by the name of Martha welcomed Him and made Him feel quite at home. She had a sister, Mary [Miriam], who sat before the Master, hanging on every word He said. But Martha was pulled away by all she had to do in the kitchen. Later, she stepped in, interrupting them. "Master, don't you care that my sister has abandoned the kitchen to me? Tell her to lend me a hand." The Master said, "Martha, dear Martha, you're fussing far too much and getting yourself worked up over nothing. One thing only is essential, and Mary has chosen it—it's the main course, and won't be taken from her." (MSG)

Miriam's humble position, at the feet of her Master reflects her inward heart and also her priorities. Her priority was seen in her undivided attention to every word that fell from the lips of her Lord. She was listening and storing every promise in her heart. Miriam is a wonderful model for us and an example to follow. How about Martha? It seems that she is very busy serving, doing, and getting everything 'just right' for her beloved visitor.

I believe Martha was a woman of deep faith and devotion to the Lord, but taking a closer look at the context it appears that Martha lost perspective about the Messiah's visit and in her serving forgot about the essence of worship. Like Martha, I sometimes find myself only giving an impression that I am serving the Lord as I do stuff for Him. I need to reexamine and ask myself, am I really worshipping Him in my heart in the midst of the activities? If I am not worshipping the One who alone is worthy to be worshipped then the activities themselves, as spiritual as they appear, whether leading music, praying with someone or cooking a meal, become hollow and burdensome.

Consider the conversation with her Messiah and Martha's words to Him, "Lord, do You not care that my sister has left me to serve alone? Therefore tell her to help me." What a question to ask the Messiah, the very One who humbled Himself to take on human flesh and was soon to pour out His life as her atonement. What kind of a heart is reflected in this statement? Questions like Martha's are mere expressions of an anxious, worried heart. A heart whose pride might be hurt by a thought that Messiah is not interested in meeting your immediate needs.

Martha, being the oldest and carrying the responsibilities that come with it, was probably used to doing much of the serving. Here with Yeshua she is expressing doubt from her worried heart, but Martha is on a roll! She proceeds to boss Yeshua around and tells Yeshua what to do when she says, "Therefore, tell her to help me."

This reflects her heart of frustration that has a touch of arrogance and pride. Where did she get the idea that she can boss around the Holy One of Israel? Don't we do the same thing when we come before God with our worried anxious hearts and begin to demand or tell God what He should do instead of sitting at His feet to listen and obey? We cannot manipulate God to get our way, but rather we should seek His grace in humility to enable us to do what we were called to do. How does Messiah respond to Martha?

> Luke 10:41, "Martha, Martha, you are worried and troubled about many things! But one thing is needed or essential. Miriam has chosen the good part, which will not be taken away from her."

We see that as Messiah says her name twice, a way to show affection and love for her and for her welfare. Then he tells Martha, "You are worried and troubled about many things."

Messiah knew that worrying is destructive. The word "anxious" translated in Luke 12:22, means "to be torn apart," and the phrase "doubtful mind," (Luke 12:29) means "to be held in suspense." It is the picture of a ship being tossed in a storm.

Understandably, we have responsibilities and duties that are more than enough to take our focus off the Messiah, the Lover of our soul. It is far more natural to worry than to worship.

WHY WORSHIP WHEN WE CAN WORRY?

Worry is deceptive. It gives us a false view of life and of God. Worry convinces us that life is made up of what we eat and what we wear. We get so concerned about the means that we totally forget about the end, which is to glorify God. Matthew 6:33-34,

"But seek first His kingdom and His righteousness; and all these things shall be added to you. Therefore do not be anxious for tomorrow; for tomorrow will care for itself. Each day has enough trouble of its own."

Worry blinds us to the world around us and the way God cares for His creation. God makes the flowers beautiful, and He even feeds the unclean ravens that have no ability to sow or reap. He ought to be able to care for men to whom He has given the ability to work. Yeshua was not suggesting that we sit around and let God feed us, for the birds work hard to stay alive. Rather, He encourages us to trust Him and cooperate with Him in using the abilities and opportunities that He gives us (2 Thessalonians 3:6-15).

How do we show people around us that we are chosen by a loving God who desires to bless us? I believe that we were created to worship our Creator, thereby displaying our loving relationship. Our worship is a testimony to those around us of the awesome God we serve.

AN INVITATION TO WORSHIP

What does it look like to worship? Do I have to come to Him dressed in my finest clothing? Do I need to sing louder than the person next to me during the worship time? In Psalm 95 we have both an invitation and instructions as to how we come to Him. It's not about our clothing, our service, our singing, or anything external. It is always a matter of the heart.

I have never received an invitation to be a guest at the White House to dine with the wife of the President at a special women's function. However, I imagine if I did receive such an invitation, the first thing I would want to know is the dress code. Is it formal, semi-formal, or business casual? Then I would want to have instructions on how to conduct myself during this auspicious occasion. But of course, I would wonder, why does the President's wife want to meet with me? Is it to have a wonderful intimate friendship or to gain political clout and get my vote in the next election?

When God extends His gracious invitation to us we can be sure it is not to gain any kind of advantage for Himself, but to develop the most intimate relationship He created us for, this intimacy through worship in His presence. In Psalm 95, God gives us a special call to worship Him.

The Creator of the Universe has already wonderfully provided our wardrobe for our summit with the King of kings as Isaiah the prophet so poetically describes. I believe this is formal wear, but there is no need to go for a fitting because this outfit is made to fit you flawlessly. It's a designer outfit by the Divine Designer that will never wear out and will be a perfect fit for eternity.

> Isaiah 61:10, "I will rejoice greatly in the LORD, My soul will exult in my God; for He has clothed me with garments of salvation, He has wrapped me with a robe of righteousness, as a bridegroom decks himself with a garland, and as a bride adorns herself with her jewels."

Psalm 95 begins, "O Come, let us sing for joy to the LORD; let us shout joyfully to the rock of our salvation." Music is definitely a part of our worship today. The children of Israel were encouraged to praise Him with both singing and instrumental praise. Verse one invites us to worship with a joyful shout or shofar blast. Please note the focus of our joyful singing and shouting; The LORD, our Covenant God, and the Rock of our Salvation, He is the One who always keeps His agreements, His covenants, and *Ketubah* with His bride. The Rock of our salvation means that our God is not only the savior, but the One who gives our lives stability and strength. Verse 2 goes on to invite us,

> "Let us come before His presence with thanksgiving;
> let us shout joyfully to Him with psalms."

When we come to worship in His presence or before His face, we are to come not with griping and complaining, but with thanksgiving and with the songs of joy. Come with enthusiasm and with thankfulness. Remember how excited you were preparing for that special event, when you were dressed up in your nicest clothes? Think of the excitement you felt in anticipation before a special evening. This is the kind of anticipation and excitement that we should have when coming before the Lord.

Verse 3 gives us the reasons as to why we should come to Him with thanksgiving and joyful songs, because He is the great God, above all others. Our God is truly the greatest; there is no one to equal Him. He is great (*gadol*). He is the King above all gods. We see the power of our great God in verses 4 and 5.

> "In His hand are the depths of the earth; the peaks of the mountains are His also. The sea is His, for it was He who made it; and His hands formed the dry land."

The Essence of Worship

We understand that He has the whole world in His hands, the lowest of places, the highest of places, and everything in between. He is our Creator God and He alone is worthy of our praise. In your life, God wants to have all your situations in His hands as you turn them over to Him. The low, depressing, disappointing, and sad circumstances as well as the places of victory and success, and then the everyday and mundane—turn them all over to Him. He can make the rough places smooth, the low places high, and the high places can all be under His control, bringing honor to Him.

FALLING FLAT ON YOUR FACE

And now in verse 6, we come to the heart of Psalm 95. Along with God's invitation to worship, there are specific instructions as to how we are to come to Him. These directives come straight from the top and tell us what kind of worship God desires from us.

> Psalm 95:6, "Oh come, let us worship and bow down: let us kneel before the Lord our God our maker."

The first word "come", *bo-u* in Hebrew, is a welcoming word, which means approach without hesitation for you will find a warm reception here. Verse 6 contains three different Hebrew words that will give us God's protocol to come before Him. The first word is "worship," *shachach* in Hebrew, which is the most common word for worship in the Scriptures. We have an example of how this word is used in the New Covenant. In Revelation 19:3-4, at the second "Hallelujah!," the Scriptures declare in verse four, "the twenty-four elders and the four living creatures fell down and worshiped God who sits on the throne saying,

"Amen. Hallelujah!" The word "worshiped" indicates that they had their faces to the ground. We find the same idea when the wise men worshiped the Messiah.

Matthew 2:2, "Where is He who has been born King of the Jews? For we saw His star in the east and have come to worship Him."

The essence of this word, *shahach*, or worship, is a picture of submission, prostration, and love. Messiah tells us of the worship that is required in John 4:24, "God is spirit, and those who worship Him must worship in spirit and truth."

However, the English word, "worship," derives its meaning from an ancient Anglo-Saxon word, "worth ship," which means to ascribe worth or value to something. When we worship God we attribute ultimate worth and value to Him. The very meaning of the word provides a question by which we can evaluate our worship. To what or to whom do we give the greatest value in our worship activities?

When we worship, do we value God above all else? Or have we come to value or give significance to our worship experiences more than the very One we are worshiping? To reiterate, this common word in Hebrew for worship is *shachach*, which describes the way we are to approach God, meaning to fall on one's face. In ancient mid-eastern culture, one person bowed to another to show that the other person had a higher social rank. The higher the other person's position, the lower one should bow. To fall on one's face indicated the highest possible distance between the social worth of the two parties. It's important for us to remember that the Hebrew Scriptures do not regard worship as a mood, but as an activity that expresses the complete superiority of God in relation to the worshiper.

At the Marriage of the Lamb, the greatest celebration of all time, there is eternal worship. We will be joining the elders and the angels who are falling on their faces to worship the Lamb of God. We will be worshipping forever with this heavenly throng. In Psalm 95:6 after "Come, let us worship," we are instructed to bow down.

A CURTSEY FOR THE KING

If one day I received an invitation to have an audience with Queen Elizabeth at her palace in London, I can only imagine receiving instructions along with the invitation regarding the proper way to acknowledge her position as queen. I would be taught that I must honor her by bowing with a curtsey motion. The phrase "to bow down" from Psalm 95 gives a similar connotation. This phrase, "bow down," is just one word in Hebrew, *kara*, and it means to acknowledge majesty and recognize sovereign rule.

If I bowed down before Queen Elizabeth with a curtsey motion it would be a mere formality to fit in with the customs of England's royalty. However with our God, the sovereign ruler of the universe, He expects this bowing down to reflect an acknowledgement of your heart. Then it is declared, affirmed, and announced publicly that He is the Lord your God.

This word, *kara*, or bow down, is used in the prophesy from Isaiah and quoted by Paul stating that "to Yeshua the Messiah every knee will bow and every tongue confess."

Isaiah 45:23, "I have sworn by Myself, The word has gone forth from My mouth in righteousness and will not turn back, that to Me every knee will bow, every tongue will swear allegiance."

Philippians 2:9-11, "God highly exalted Him, and bestowed on Him the name which is above every name, so that at the name of Yeshua every knee will bow, of those who are in heaven and on earth and under the earth, and that every tongue will confess that Yeshua the Messiah is Lord, to the glory of God the Father."

We can anticipate this future global acknowledgement of the awesome majesty of Yeshua the Messiah, the King of Glory. Today it is our privilege to reveal and manifest God's character in our lives that honors Him as our Lord. To recap, worship is both a prostration before the Lord and bowing down to Him.

The third phrase, "Let us kneel," gives us another aspect of what it means to come before the LORD in worship. The word for "knee" in Hebrew is *barek*. The commonly used word, "bless," or *baruch*, is derived from *barek* or knee. Here we have another clue about the physical position of the worshipper as well as the position of our hearts which are to be yielded to Him as we bend the knee in His presence.

This word, "bless," or *baruch*, is a word that begins most liturgical prayers in Jewish life. For example, "Blessed are You O Lord our God King of the universe" (*Baruch Atah Adonai Eloheynu Melech Ha Olam*).

The apostle Paul, a Jewish believer, would have been accustomed to beginning these familiar Jewish prayers with the words, "Blessed are Thou." In fact, Paul begins his letter to the believers at Ephesus with this traditional phrase, "Blessed be the God and Father of our Lord Yeshua the Messiah, who has blessed us with every spiritual blessing in the heavenly places in Messiah" (Ephesians 1:3).

In this prayer, Paul is acknowledging what God has done for each one of us. He blesses the Lord by ascribing Him worth. This speaks of the idea that when we bend the knee and humble ourselves before our Holy God, we are blessing Him by acknowledging what He has done on our behalf. Our yielded lives reflect our praise and gratefulness to Him.

A HEART FOR WORSHIP

Today, as we practice the protocol of worship before the King, it seems clear. Scripture teaches us that worship is much more than simply an emotional or intellectual experience. At the heart of the matter, worship is about God. It is a physical expression of the worshiper's highest values. It is the obedient response to God of those of us who acknowledge Him to be the sovereign Lord of our lives and of the universe. If the heart of the matter is worship, then we must understand that all our spiritual activity emanates from the heart. That includes the inner person, the mind, and the will. The heart is the home of my personal life, as Messiah taught us.

> Matthew 15:18-19, "But the things that proceed out of the mouth come from the heart, and those defile

the man. For out of the heart come evil thoughts, murders, adulteries, fornications, thefts, false witness, slanders."

The prophet Ezekiel put it this way:

> Ezekiel 36:25-27, "Then I will sprinkle clean water on you, and you will be clean; I will cleanse you from all your filthiness and from all your idols. Moreover, I will give you a new heart and put a new spirit within you; and I will remove the heart of stone from your flesh and give you a heart of flesh. I will put My Spirit within you and cause you to walk in My statutes."

These Scriptures teach us that we are unable to worship without a new heart. King David prayed that God would create in Him a pure or clean heart (Psalm 51:10). The wisest man who ever lived, King Solomon, had heart troubles which were his demise in his later years.

> 1 Kings 11:4, "For it came about when Solomon was old, his wives turned his heart away after other gods; and his heart was not wholly devoted to the LORD his God, as the heart of David his father had been."

The distractions of his life turned his heart away from worshipping the One True God. It led him in a downward spiral which ultimately turned his heart away from the Lord.

"Watch over your heart with all diligence, for from it flow the springs (or beginnings) of life." Proverbs 4:23.

No one can worship the Lord in defiance or pride. We must come to Him in humility, acknowledging that we are totally dependent (like the sheep of His hand) on what He alone can give. As we worship, we must yield our hearts to Him, bow down at His feet, and bless the Lord. Then we will find the intimacy and understand the purpose of our lives. We cannot understand God's choosing us in love without an intimate life of worship. I was blessed through studying this Psalm and wrote a song with the chorus in Hebrew to express my heart:

Bo-u, Bo-u, nish tach ha vey Bo-u v' neech-ra-ah
Bo-u neev-r-cha lifneh haShem oseynu
Lifneh HaShem oseynu

Oh Come, oh come to worship the King
Oh Come bow down to Him
Oh Come and kneel before the LORD our maker
Before the LORD our maker. (repeat)

Come with exuberant song
Accept with thanks His gracious invitation
Join with the heavenly throng
Shout with joy to the rock of our salvation

Give your heart to Messiah,
Worship HaShem the King above all kings
He alone, He is worthy,
And to His Name all our praises we bring.

I pray that this study will give us inspiration to continually see ourselves as His Chosen Bride and live in eager anticipation of His return. We live each day with the understanding that what we do matters, and staying close to Him through worship and the study of His Word.

QUESTIONS AND REFLECTIONS:

1. Write out your definition of Worship.

2. Who do you identify most with—Martha or Miriam? Both were loved by Yeshua (John 11:5) and both women were deeply spiritual. Consider not only Miriam at the feet of Yeshua but Martha's response to Him in John 11: 21-18

3. Do you tend to be a worrier? If so write down what causes you worry and be afraid so you can ask God to help you in these areas.

4. Consider your heart and ask God to reveal anything that would hinder you from truly worshipping your Groom and King.

If you would like to contact us, please contact:

miriam@wordofmessiah.org

Book layout and Cover Design
by Natalia Fomin

Eternally Desired by Miriam Nadler

© 2014, 2017 by Miriam Nadler and Natalia Fomin
All Rights Reserved
Printed in United States of America
ISBN: 978-1-5058112

Made in the USA
Middletown, DE
19 June 2019